Raising Good Sons

**Other Books by Julie Lavender**

*Children's Bible Stories for Bedtime*

*Strength for All Seasons: A Mom's Devotional
of Powerful Verses and Prayers*

# RAISING GOOD SONS

CHRISTIAN | *for Nurturing*
PARENTING | *Boys of Faith*
PRINCIPLES | *and Character*

**DAVID & JULIE LAVENDER**

ZEITGEIST · NEW YORK

*To our four children,*

*Jeremy, Jenifer, Jeb, and Jessica.*

*We're so proud of the amazing*

*men and women you've become—*

*young adults with strong faith and*

*good character. It's our greatest honor*

*and blessing to be your parents!*

# CONTENTS

# INTRODUCTION

Welcome, parents and guardians of boys. What an honor it is to be chosen by God to raise and nurture precious boys, from infant to adult. God is counting on you to bring up his boys according to his plan, ensuring your boy's faith and relationship with Jesus.

Let's face it—parenting boys is no easy task! On some days, you may feel like you've accomplished the task if they are fed, clothed, and asleep by bedtime. But beyond meeting their physical needs, God calls us to much more. The responsibilities of Christian parents raising boys include modeling godly character, practicing strong faith, teaching respect, and showing love.

We, the authors, raised two sons and two daughters. All four are godly adults, and we've welcomed two godly sons-in-love and three grandchildren. We don't profess to have all the answers by any means! What we share in the pages of this book worked for us by the grace of God, his guidance, answered prayers, blessings, and much help from extended family, pastors and ministers, Christian friends, and neighbors.

As parents we put our life in his hands and trusted him to lead. We trusted the Holy Spirit, spent much time in prayer, surrounded ourselves with godly influences, and recognized that no child ever comes with an instruction manual. And, even if they did, we'd have to throw that one out and get a new one with the next child!

A lot of good parenting materials are available from child experts, and great advice will come from well-meaning family and friends. We're blessed in this age of technology to have parenting resources at the tip of our fingers. But as we choose information to follow, we must remember first the parenting principles that God, the ultimate parent, passed on to us to nurture and guide our children. This book is filled with Scripture and the lessons and truths that God wants parents to live by.

Biblical parenting means raising our boys with God's truths and values as our guide. Our goal is to help our boys develop a personal relationship and saving faith in Jesus Christ and put God at the center of their lives. Biblical parenting is a lifelong journey, and the weight of that responsibility is not to be taken lightly.

Sometimes we overlook God's Word and voice in this noisy, distracting world. Thanks to Uncle Sam, my husband and I have lived in a dozen homes in six states. That's a lot of distractions! Unfortunately, in one or two of those zip codes, we sometimes let the busyness of life interfere with our walk and hinder the strong faith we hoped to impart to our children, while others demanded deeper faith due to difficult struggles. Sometimes we got it right; other times we didn't. But we always found our way back to God amid the day-to-day challenges. With God's help, we raised precious boys who became men of strong faith and character.

We hope this book will help parents and guardians of boys lean on God. Whether your son is an infant, toddler, or teen, this book is filled with principles and biblical lessons you can rely on. With God and faith, you'll never be lost or alone in this parenting journey. Hang on to God. He won't ever let you down.

# TRAIN UP YOUR SON

TEACHING YOUR SON basic spiritual truths helps him make an informed decision about accepting Christ. The accountability for our sons' spiritual and moral teaching lies with us—parents or guardians. Not our church nor a Christian or public school and not even neighbors, friends, or community. *We* hold that responsibility. And let's face it—it's a huge obligation. An obligation that we can't afford to treat lightly. Yet it's also a privilege and a joy to raise your son with intentionality to guide him toward Jesus.

Training up your son means more than meeting physical needs. The goal at the very heart and soul of your parenting tasks—to train him to love Jesus—meets his spiritual needs and secures his future eternally.

Proverbs 22:6 (NKJV) says, "Train up a child in the way he should go, and when he is old he will not depart from it." Starting from infancy, age appropriately of course, you can train up your son to honor God, follow Jesus, trust the Holy Spirit, and believe the Bible—spiritual truths that lead him on a pathway to a personal decision about accepting Christ.

Be intentional to impart basic spiritual truths for your son to stamp on his heart and etch in his mind, so that young or old, he'll not depart from them.

## Honor God

*To love the LORD your God, to walk in obedience to him, to keep his commands, to hold fast to him and to serve him with all your heart and with all your soul.* JOSHUA 22:5B (NIV)

To serve God with *all* our heart and soul implies God should be first in every aspect of our lives. We honor God when we put him first in everything. Practically and biblically speaking, we honor God when we love and obey him, when we keep his commands, when we hang on to him as the essence of our very being, and when we serve him with heart and soul.

We can and should honor God with our thoughts and words, with our actions both in public and private, and with our time.

Our oldest son, Jeremy, enjoyed singing with the youth praise team as a middle schooler. The team consisted of five or six students, a blend of singers and musicians. Most of the time, the band gelled, focused on the Lord, and led the youth in worship and praise with spiritual maturity.

One particular week, team members bickered over who should be the lead singer, which musician got a solo spot, and how many songs needed the drummer's intro. Jeremy just wanted everyone happy, but when it dawned on him that the team's actions were not honoring God, he emailed band members to share his thoughts. "I think we're letting pride get in our way," Jeremy said. "This isn't about us. We're not putting God first with the way we're acting. I think we can do better."

Jeremy's friends agreed. They changed their tune—literally—and honored God fittingly.

God commands—and deserves—glory and honor. Always.

## Biblical Lessons in Action

- We can honor God with our actions, prayers, worship, thoughts, tithes, and more. What's your favorite? Which one helps you feel closest to God? Is there one that's out of your comfort zone you could work on with your son?
- Think of someone you know who excels at honoring God. What stands out most in your mind as God-honoring qualities? How can you incorporate those actions and attitudes with your son?
- What ways was God honored (or not) in your home growing up? Which would you like to emulate, and which would you want to change?

- How do you model honoring God on a daily basis to your son? What parts of that honoring spirit do you do well, and what parts could use improvement?

## PRAYER

Dear God, help me love and honor you with my heart, my soul, and my mind. Help me practice honoring you so faithfully that it becomes a natural and treasured habit, one that my son will willingly choose to emulate. Help me train my son to honor you. Amen.

## Follow Jesus

*Jesus said to him, "I am the way, the truth, and the life. No one comes to the Father except through Me."* JOHN 14:6 (NKJV)

Running late, we rushed to the sanctuary with the kids in hopes of slipping into a back pew. From the overhead speaker in the foyer, we heard the worship leader announce the next song by quoting the first line: "Open our eyes, Lord. We want to see Jesus." Four-year-old Jeb Daniel tugged my hand and said, "Mommy, we get to see Jesus today!"

I squeezed his hand, gave him a wink, and whispered softly, "I pray you forever keep the sparkle I see in your eyes at this moment, my sweet son."

Teaching truths about Jesus with your son is a precursor to his forever walk with Christ. Helping your son learn from the Bible about Jesus' birth, childhood (though only briefly recorded), ministry, sacrifice, death, resurrection, and role in the Trinity takes your son closer to his own personal relationship with Jesus.

Start with the basics if your son is young and gradually move to deeper thoughts as he matures. Read stories about Jesus from the New Testament, but make sure your son sees the thread of God's promise of a Savior that's woven throughout the Old Testament, too.

Sharing openly about your personal relationship with Christ further solidifies the truths your son grasps from God's Word, the Bible, and helps him see how what he's learning in the Bible can be lived out in life. And hopefully that same sparkle in your eyes will entice him to follow Jesus, also—our ultimate goal.

Make sure your son sees Jesus—the way and the truth that leads to eternal life with the Father.

## Biblical Lessons in Action

- How was your life visibly different after you made a decision to follow Jesus? Are there habits, word choices, actions, or thoughts that you might yet need to work on that would be more pleasing to God?

- In a message about the birth of Jesus quoted in Isaiah 9:6b (NKJV), Isaiah the prophet said Jesus would be called "Wonderful, Counselor, Mighty God, Everlasting Father, Prince of Peace." Which one of those names resonates most with you in this season of life and why? Review those names with your son and find out his favorite, too.
- Search online for "names of Jesus in the Bible." Which name gives you the most comfort and peace as a parent?

## PRAYER

Dear God, your Word tells me Jesus is called "the Bread of Life," "Redeemer," "Lamb of God," "Alpha and Omega," and other powerful names. Thank you for being my beginning and end, my Savior, and the very sustenance of my existence. Please let my son see Jesus in me. Amen.

## Trust the Holy Spirit

*But the Helper, the Holy Spirit whom the Father will send in My name, He will teach you all things, and remind you of all that I said to you.* JOHN 14:26 (NASB)

Scripture reveals the role of the Holy Spirit as helper and teacher. Once we receive Jesus as our Savior, the Holy Spirit resides in our heart forever, to guide our thoughts and actions and prayers, to teach us about God when we study the Bible, to convict us of wrongdoing, and to help us grow to be more like Jesus.

You can help your son understand that once the Holy Spirit takes up residence in our hearts, he never leaves us. We can always count on the Holy Spirit's help and guidance: to choose right from wrong, to know how to treat others, to choose healthy relationships, to make important life decisions, to know what we should and shouldn't do, and to help us discern the heart of others.

When we lived in California, eight-year-old Jeremy made friends with the ten-year-old across the street, who unfortunately soon revealed bullying tendencies, sometimes directed at Jeb Daniel, our younger son. Jeremy's anger spilled over as a first reaction. We reminded Jeremy to pray for Walter, but in all honesty, my wife and I seethed with our own anger, especially when Jeremy revealed Walter encouraged him to bully other neighborhood kids.

The next time Walter wanted to play, Jeremy politely refused. "I'll pray for him, Daddy, but I don't think I should spend time with him."

"That's the Holy Spirit helping you make wise choices, Jeremy," I pointed out. "We can always trust his guidance."

Trust the Holy Spirit! He'll never steer you wrong.

# Biblical Lessons in Action

- Share a time you felt the Holy Spirit leading you. What did the Holy Spirit reveal to you? Share specifics of a time the Holy Spirit guided you in an important decision. When have you felt the Holy Spirit's conviction?
- How can you help your son understand the role of the Holy Spirit as part of the Trinity and as a vital part of his relationship with Jesus?
- In the book of Romans, the Bible tells us the Holy Spirit groans prayers on our behalf when we can't find the words to say. Discuss a recent time you were thankful for the Holy Spirit's groaning.
- How does confidence that the Holy Spirit resides in you give you the strength to face a difficult parenting situation?

## PRAYER

Dear God, thank you for sending the Holy Spirit to help, guide, and convict me. Teach me more about you through the Holy Spirit's guidance. Help me be more like Jesus through the Holy Spirit's teaching. Show me how to adequately teach my son about the Holy Spirit. Amen.

# Believe the Bible

*How can a young person stay on the path of purity? By living according to your word. I seek you with all my heart; do not let me stray from your commands.* PSALM 119:9–10 (NIV)

Jeremy was reading the Bible when he came across a passage he felt led to share with the youth minister, who was Jeremy's mentor, special friend, and one of two bald pastors on staff.

At the next youth event, Pastor Tony mentioned Jeremy and shared this passage from 2 Kings 2:23–24 (NIV): "From there Elisha went up to Bethel. As he was walking along the road, some boys came out of the town and jeered at him. 'Get out of here, baldy!' they said. 'Get out of here, baldy!' He turned around, looked at them and called down a curse on them in the name of the Lord. Then two bears came out of the woods and mauled forty-two of the boys."

The students caught the connection between their bald pastor and bald Elisha, but they doubted the validity of the story. "No way—that's not in the Bible," said one. "I've never heard *that* story," said another. They vowed to read the rest of the story for themselves.

Just because most of the students had never heard the story of a bald prophet, jeering teens, and mauling bears didn't make it untrue. The Holy Bible is the inerrant, inspired Word of God. We can trust and believe every word. God speaks to us today through his words in the Bible. Everything we need to know about God, accepting Christ as Savior, life on this side of heaven, and eternal life is found between the pages of Genesis and Revelation.

## Biblical Lessons in Action

- Which one of God's promises from the Bible is especially important to you? Are there some parts of the Bible that are more difficult for you to believe? Why do you think that's so?
- Does your son have a Bible of his own? Do you encourage him to read the Bible daily? What practical steps can you take to help him believe every word in the Bible?
- Give your son a journal and encourage him to complete this sentence in relation to what he reads: "I believe the Bible is true because . . ."
- How does the Bible help you stay on the path of purity? How can you help your son seek God and build a personal relationship with Jesus by reading the Bible?

### PRAYER

Lord, thank you for your living, breathing Word. Let me never tire of reading the Bible. Give me strength to live according to your instructions and seek you continuously. Please help my son have a hunger for your Word. Help him believe every chapter, verse, and word is inspired by you. Amen.

## PARENTING PRINCIPLE 2 | POINT HIM TO JESUS

YOUR MOST IMPORTANT daily responsibility as a parent is to point your son toward Christ—to deliberately keep him focused on Jesus with his eyes, mind, and heart. You can encourage this focus by consistently involving your son in church, helping him stay in God's Word, talking about God often, and practicing praise and adoration for our Heavenly Father.

You have the blessed opportunity to lead your son closer to Christ with each day, each activity, each conversation. When you show him how to connect every part of life with Christ, you help your son take another step closer to him.

Saying grace before a meal points to Jesus as the provider of every good gift. Praying before bedtime reminds your son of God's provision and protection throughout the day. Reading the Bible regularly keeps God's Word fresh, living, and active in your son's heart and mind. It's all about him—Jesus—and the more you instill that in your son's heart, the closer he moves to a personal relationship with Christ.

When you encourage your son's walk with Christ, you can echo John's words in 3 John 1:4 (NIV): "I have no greater joy than to hear that my children are walking in the truth."

## Involve Him in Church

*Let us not neglect meeting together, as some have made a habit, but let us encourage one another.* HEBREWS 10:25A (BSB)

We'd recently moved to Oceanside, California. As my wife and I nudged our kids toward the car, I casually mentioned the name of the fifth church we planned to visit. One more option in a long list of possibilities in the San Diego area.

Jeremy, eight at the time, sighed. "Can we please go to the same church two Sundays in a row?"

My son recognized what I didn't. He missed the fellowship of our previous church. Indecisiveness about a place for worship took precious time away from our immersion in a new church family.

The Bible instructs us in Hebrews 10:25 to "hang out"—my paraphrase—with other believers. This life is tough, and even tougher if we try to go it alone without the support of Christian friends and family.

Make sure your son is involved in corporate worship, as well as other small groups like connect groups or Sunday school,

Vacation Bible School, choir, youth gatherings, church-wide mission opportunities, and other events. Church activities build a sense of belonging and community and open the door for spiritual conversations.

Participate with your son at every opportunity and discuss each event. Talk about the sermon. Ask what he learned in Sunday school. Sing familiar worship songs in the car. Talk about the "why" of a missions opportunity.

Regular church involvement teaches us to live in fellowship with other believers, immerses us in the love of God, and ultimately points us toward Jesus—right where we want our sons to be!

## Biblical Lessons in Action

- Being involved in church allows your son to learn more about Jesus and your Christian community. Do you have a favorite childhood church memory? If so, share it with your son and encourage him to make his own favorite church memories.
- What church activities do you and your son take part in? Any others you'd like to try? How have these activities furthered your walk with Jesus? How about your son's faith journey?
- Going to church isn't about trying to earn God's love. He already loves us more than we could ever imagine. What part of being involved in a local church helps you feel God's love and presence?
- How will you encourage spiritual conversations with your son after time spent at church?

## Stay in God's Word

*Let the word of Christ dwell in you richly, teaching and admonishing one another in all wisdom, singing psalms and hymns and spiritual songs, with thankfulness in your hearts to God.* COLOSSIANS 3:16 (ESV)

An obvious but sometimes overlooked way to point your son to Jesus is to stay in God's Word. Read the Bible regularly for your own personal spiritual growth and encourage your son to do the same. Children's Bibles abound, geared toward all ages and stages. From toddler to youth to college to adult—God's Word is available to fit the needs of your son at any age.

Start reading to your son long before he understands the words or stories. Make it a habit to encourage a hunger for God's Word. With younger boys, snuggle on the couch every night before bed-time or start the morning with a Bible story. Keep it consistent!

Make Bible-reading time enjoyable, too. Read with enthusiasm and various voice inflections to make the story come to life. Add story-related crafts, coloring pages, or made-up songs. Ask questions to solidify biblical truths. Act out stories with your son's toys. Have conversations at mealtimes about recently read Bible stories. Memorize Scripture together in fun ways, like chants or songs with familiar tunes.

Keep your son immersed in God's Word. Once he becomes a proficient reader, encourage his own Bible-reading time with an age-appropriate Bible, but don't forgo reading God's Word together with follow-up conversations.

Help your son understand the importance of God's Word. It's how he speaks to us. It's how he gives us instructions to know how to love him and glorify him with our lives. Keeping your son in God's Word points him to Jesus.

## Biblical Lessons in Action

- Do you have a favorite spot in the house to read your Bible? Where's your favorite place to read God's Word to your son? When does your son seem most eager to hear God's Word, in the morning, evening, or some other time?
- What's your favorite way to make Bible reading fun for your son? Do you have a regular Bible reading plan?
- How does your son seem to internalize and absorb Bible stories best: with follow-up questions, a related craft project, a song about the story, or an open-ended discussion?

- How can you encourage your son to memorize Scripture? What method of Scripture memorization works best with your son? Repetition? Writing it out on note cards to post in his room?

## PRAYER

Dear God, help me fall more deeply in love with your Word with each treasured Bible story and passage I read. Let my enthusiasm for the Bible be evident to my son. Fill him with a hunger for your Word and point him to your Son with each passage he reads. Amen.

## Talk About God Often

*You shall also teach them to your sons, speaking of them when you sit in your house, when you walk along the road, when you lie down, and when you get up.* DEUTERONOMY 11:19 (NASB)

While watching a short animated show with my five-year-old grandson, I asked him a question about the size of the pink puppy character. "Well, Grandmommy," Benaiah said. "That's just the way God made him."

We didn't get into a discussion about real versus imaginary, but I couldn't help but chuckle at his quick response. When we talk about God often with our sons, or grandsons, God is always the answer!

The Bible encourages us to talk about God's words when we sit, walk, lie down, and get up—in other words—*all the time*! Let God be the focus of your conversation. Keep him at the center.

Call attention to God's creation. Teach your son to observe God's beauty in nature. Relate current events to stories in the Bible. Share applications from familiar Bible stories to daily life happenings.

Help your son make decisions based on what he knows about God's character and God's desires. Teach your son to pray through decisions, challenging situations, upcoming tests, friendships, job searches, career choices, and so much more. And teach him to pray for others, too.

Talk about God's character, his goodness, his promises, his faithfulness, and his strong love. Emphasize God's great love for your son in that he sent his Son Jesus to make a way for us to live eternally with God in heaven. Keep God in the forefront of your son's thoughts such that everything he does or encounters reminds him of God, and God is always the right answer!

## Biblical Lessons in Action

- Did your parents openly talk about God when you were growing up? Did their conversations and actions point you to Jesus? If the answer is *yes*, how can you do something similar? If the answer is *no*, how can you make a concerted effort to faithfully talk about God and Jesus with your son?

- What visual reminder can you use outdoors to talk about God with your son? How can God's creation initiate conversations about Jesus?
- How can you talk about God when you're doing chores with your son? Making dinner? Running errands? When your son has a friend over?
- Has your son ever started a conversation about God without your leading? What prompted the discussion?

## PRAYER

Dearest Heavenly Father, thank you for your great love for me and my son. Help me see you in everything I do and in everything that surrounds me. Please give me the right words to talk about you with my son, words that point him to Jesus. Amen.

## Practice Praise and Adoration

*I will give thanks to the LORD with all my heart; I will recount all Your wonders. I will be glad and rejoice in You; I will sing praise to Your name, O Most High.* PSALM 9:1–2 (BSB)

Have you ever thought about the difference between "praise" and "adoration"? I really hadn't when my boys were younger, and I'll admit I didn't do a good job of teaching them to express adoration until much later. In fact, they were young adults when I began to emphasize adoration more in my prayer time.

Now, I try to start my quiet time of prayer with adoration before jumping into my laundry list of requests. I often begin: "Good morning, Lord. You are holy and perfect and good." Or, "Dear Jesus, I adore you. You are sinless, blameless, compassionate, and kind. There is no one else like you."

Stating words of adoration aloud in our prayer time helps us recognize the magnificence of God as well as Jesus' sacrifice on our behalf. Pointing us to Jesus, words of adoration place our heart in a reverent, right mode for prayer.

As your son gets older, you might choose to teach him the ACTS way to pray: Adoration, Confession, Thanksgiving, and Supplication. Help him start with adoration—worshiping and praising God for who he is and what he has done and addressing his always-good character. Next, encourage your son to confess sins and wrongdoings.

Then comes my favorite part of prayer—praise! Encourage your son to give thanks to God, expressing gratitude for all he has done. And last in this method of praying, supplication—making our requests known to God. Help your son learn to pray for others and for himself.

# Biblical Lessons in Action

- How do you (or can you) include praise and adoration in your prayer time? How can you encourage your son to include praise and adoration in his prayer time?
- Are you a pray-er who follows a self-imposed guideline and specific order when you pray? Or do you pray in a more random, sporadic fashion? Don't worry—God loves all our conversations with him. Have you thought about praying in a different way than "normal" for you?
- What part of Jesus' character do you most enjoy praising? Why?
- Search online for "names of God and their meaning." Consider incorporating different names in your prayers of adoration and model those prayers for your son.

## PRAYER

Dear Jesus, you truly are holy and perfect and good and there is no one else like you. Let words of adoration fill my heart and flow from my mouth. Please make yourself known to my son so that he'll be filled with words of adoration, too. We love you, Jesus. Amen.

# PARENTING PRINCIPLE 3 | PRAY WITHOUT CEASING

SPECIFIC PRAYER BY you, your son, and anyone else you can enlist is a key component of your son's faith walk. The apostle Paul emphasized the importance of prayer in Ephesians 6:18 (NLT), writing, "Pray in the Spirit at all times and on every occasion. Stay alert and be persistent in your prayers for all believers everywhere." Paul also admonished, "Pray without ceasing," in 1 Thessalonians 5:17 (ESV).

Stated quite simply, prayer is conversation with God. However, nothing about prayer can ever be minimized. Prayer is our powerful means of connecting with God. Prayer, for your children, for your parenting journey, with your children, and with your parenting partner, draws us into relationship with God.

Teaching your son to pray without ceasing encourages him to make prayer a priority and to pray often and diligently. Incessant prayer mode gives us an awareness of God's continuous presence and helps us turn to him in scary situations or during difficult tasks. That same God-conscious posture also helps us recognize God's grace and blessings and implores us to give God the credit he's due with praise and thanksgiving, rather than basking in our own accomplishments.

Knowing *about* God is not the same for your son as knowing God personally. Encouraging your son to pray without ceasing nurtures his relationship with God and points him to Jesus.

## Pray for Your Children

*Do not be anxious about anything, but in every situation, by prayer and petition, with thanksgiving, present your requests to God.* PHILIPPIANS 4:6 (NIV)

When my oldest son, Jeremy, was a college student on the West Coast, he drove across the country for Christmas at our home in Georgia. He encountered a sudden snowstorm late in the evening. He used his hands-free device to update me frequently, but spotty service caused each call to drop mid-sentence. This mama's heart skipped a beat with each dropped call. I spent the next two hours in prayer as he crept along the roadway toward safety.

Praying for your son, at any age or stage, and making your son aware of those prayers, strengthens his faith right along with yours. With every answered prayer, trust builds and confidence in God's answers soars, for you and your son. Sometimes the answer may be *yes*, sometimes *no*, and sometimes *not right now but wait patiently*. But regardless of God's answer, your son learns the importance and power of prayer and a praying parent.

Begin praying for your son long before birth, but definitely dive into conversation with God about your son as an infant. Some life events you might pray for include your son's health, growth and development, emotional development, academic success, friendships, teachers, education, career, and future spouse and family.

Most importantly, pray for your son's personal relationship with Christ. Ask God to give him wisdom for what comes his way and the strength to withstand temptation and sin. Plead with God for safety and provision for your son.

Encourage your son's faith walk with your continuous prayers.

## Biblical Lessons in Action

- How often do you pray for your son throughout the day in addition to your regularly scheduled quiet time? What prompts you to pray for your son during those times?
- Do you remember to thank God frequently for your son? Do you remember to tell your son that you thank God for him? Make a habit of doing just that to remind your son how much you love him and how grateful you are that he's part of your family.
- Consider keeping a prayer journal with specific prayer requests for your son. Use different colored markers to highlight requests and praises. You might want to use different colors

for school-related requests, family-related ones, extracurricular activities, and long-range prayer requests, like advanced education and career choices.

## PRAYER

Dear God, thank you for the gift of my son. Protect and guide him and draw him to you. Strengthen his faith and trust in you through my prayers for him and build my faith and trust, too. I'm so grateful you hear every one of my prayers. I love you, God. Amen.

## Pray for Your Parenting Journey

*Therefore I tell you, whatever you ask for in prayer, believe that you have received it, and it will be yours.* MARK 11:24 (NIV)

David received orders for a duty station in Virginia the summer before Jeremy started second grade. I'd made the decision to homeschool him for kindergarten and first grade partly because I wanted more time with him before enrolling him in school and partly because the school district we were in struggled with overcrowded classrooms and teacher shortages.

As a former schoolteacher, I was a huge proponent of public school systems and planned to support the recently built elementary school in our new neighborhood. However, I waffled with the decision once we settled in. Busily unpacking cartons and boxes, I failed to pray about the school situation. When I fervently turned to the Lord in prayer, God revealed to me his desire for us to continue homeschooling, and I finally felt a deep sense of peace. I'm still a huge supporter of public education, but homeschooling was the right decision for our family with frequent military moves.

I learned an important lesson about praying for every aspect of my parenting journey during that time. No detail is too small for God's concern, and no detail is too big for him to handle. God wants me to take my cares to him through prayer. When I pray without ceasing, I lean into God and depend on him to hear my prayers and answer them in his timing and in his will.

Praying for your parenting journey and sharing those prayers with your son strengthens your son's faith and fortifies his relationship with our loving God.

## Biblical Lessons in Action

- What part or parts of your parenting journey do you find to be the most challenging or most stressful? Do you regularly bring these situations to the Lord in prayer?
- How does it comfort you to know that God cares about every detail of your parenting journey? How does that concern make it easier for you to approach him in prayer with each aspect of your journey?

- Think about a particular situation with parenting your son where God answered your prayer in a mighty way. Who, besides your son, can you share that story with to strengthen their faith and trust in the Lord?
- As a busy mom or dad, how can you "pray without ceasing" for your parenting journey throughout the day?

## PRAYER

Dear Father, this parenting journey is not easy at times. In fact, it's downright difficult during many seasons! Please help me turn to you with my cares and concerns and worship you with my praises and adoration. Help me pray without ceasing and help me teach my son to do the same. Amen.

## Pray with Your Children

*This is the confidence we have in approaching God: that if we ask anything according to his will, he hears us.* 1 JOHN 5:14 (NIV)

Modeling prayer with your son from an early age lays the foundation for his own faithful prayer walk. Watching us pray can have a huge impact on our toddler's future relationship with the Lord.

- Pray with your son consistently to set the stage for his own prayers. Here are a few tips to instill the practice of a vibrant prayer life in your son. Establish a quiet time routine where you help your son pray regularly and with focus. Encourage him also to express short prayers throughout the day, like prayers of thanksgiving for a rainbow in the sky or requests for wisdom just before a test or exam.
- Pray with your son in the morning before he leaves for school, at bedtime, and before meals, encouraging him to give thanks for God's provisions and to request help for those who are hungry.
- Help your son learn that prayer time is the avenue to a strong, healthy relationship with God. Consistent prayer helps us discern God's will and follow God's path. And regular prayer time can lead your son's heart to a personal relationship with Jesus.

When our kids were young, David and I argued over who would pray with our second-born, Jenifer. Jokingly, of course, because prayer time with our kids was and is always sweet. Whereas Jeremy's prayers were focused and to the point, precious Jenifer prayed for socks and friends. As young adults, each of our children shares a healthy relationship with Jesus. I'm thankful it may have begun with prayers for socks.

# Biblical Lessons in Action

- How has consistent and regular prayer time affected your faith walk? What evidence of a stronger faith have you witnessed through prayers? How does talking with God build trust and strengthen your relationship with him?
- How can praying with your son strengthen his faith? How have your son's prayers changed over the years? How have your prayers changed over the years?
- Remember secret handshakes and coded signals? Talk with your son and brainstorm a special signal between the two of you that means "let's pray about that." Consider a raised index finger or touching an eyebrow with a pinkie finger. When something happens that needs immediate prayer yet you'd rather talk about it later, make eye contact, exhibit the secret signal, and silently pray.

## PRAYER

Dear God, thank you for the confidence to approach you in prayer with anything that concerns me. Thank you for answering my prayers contingent upon your will, because you know what's best for me and my son. Thank you for sending Jesus so that I can have a personal relationship with you. Amen.

# Pray with Your Parenting Partner

*Again I say to you, if two of you agree on earth about anything they ask, it will be done for them by my Father in heaven.* MATTHEW 18:19 (ESV)

Some of our dear friends in Jacksonville, Florida, had three boys and lived just across the street from us in base housing. She once shared that she and her husband prayed together every night and most prayers centered around their three boys. I'll admit, though David and I prayed together often, our busyness seemed to keep us from making it a regular habit. We did better with personal prayer time and grace before meals.

But watching her relationship with her husband and three boys, I was convicted to work harder to make prayer time with David an active part of our faith walk. And, boy, did it make a difference in our family dynamics! Praying with the father of my children helped us focus on what was best for our family with each choice we made. Praying together kept us on the same page with boundaries for our kids and financial decisions.

Praying together strengthened our relationship with God and solidified our own relationship. We treasure our prayer times together, and we seem to be more in tune with God's blessings, answers, and guidance when we pray as a united front for our family.

Praying without ceasing with your parenting partner can help you strive to be holy and pure and more like Jesus. Even if your son's other parent is unwilling or unavailable to pray with you, you can request other godly people to join with you in prayer for your son. When you remind your son that you pray together as his parents or when you pray together in front of your son, you encourage his faith walk and affirm the importance and power of praying parents.

## Biblical Lessons in Action

- Whether married, divorced, single, or separated, do you find a way to pray often with your parenting partner for your son? That may present quite a challenge. If it is too difficult to pray with an estranged parenting partner, make a habit of praying for that person and remind your son often that you do so.
- How has praying together brought you closer to your spouse? What differences do you see in your family life and marriage relationship that are a direct result of praying together?
- How does praying together help you become a better parent? In what ways can you improve prayer time with your parenting partner?

## PRAYER

Dear God, you know our situation and the particular challenges of it. Thank you for the people in my son's life who love and pray for him. Help me raise my son to grow up to love Jesus and worship you. Show me how to love you even more. Amen.

# CULTIVATE AN ATTITUDE OF GRATITUDE

BEING GRATEFUL TO God for his blessings is vital for your son to grow in faith, and it's never too early nor too late to teach the art of gratitude. Gratitude means recognizing God's goodness and has nothing to do with material possessions, wealth, or status. Gratitude is an outward expression of our thankfulness for who God is and what he's done for us. God's work through Christ's sacrifice on the cross should captivate us with such awe-inspiring wonder and thanksgiving that we can't help but have an attitude of gratitude.

Kids (and many adults) aren't naturally grateful. In fact, we're often self-centered and entitled. Gratitude takes practice and effort. First Thessalonians 5:18 (ESV) says, "Give thanks in all circumstances; for this is the will of God in Christ Jesus for you."

A life that lacks gratitude takes our focus off Christ and puts the focus on ourselves—our wants and needs. We tend to dwell on what we don't have instead of recognizing the many gifts—tangible and intangible—that God has given us.

Help your son cultivate an attitude of gratitude that includes thanking God, recognizing Jesus' sacrifice, counting blessings, and staying strong during tough times. Your son's grateful heart has the potential to strengthen his faith when his focus remains on Christ and God's goodness.

## Give Thanks to God

*But thanks be to God, who gives us the victory through our Lord Jesus Christ.* 1 CORINTHIANS 15:57 (ESV)

My daughter recorded an audio of my five-year-old grandson singing in the shower. He belted out these words: "I am so happy, so *berry* happy. I have the love of Jesus in my heart. I have been so happy. I have the love of Jesus in my heart." Though he added some words, his grammar was off, and he missed a note or two, he sang the most perfect tune any of us could desire.

To have the love of Jesus in our heart.

Teach your son to give thanks to God and start with his Son, Jesus. What a special gift we have in the person of Jesus! No matter what happens, we have the victory because of Jesus. The battle is already won. Christ reigns victorious, and we can thank God for his Son.

You can help your son recognize he may not always feel grateful due to tough times or a bad day. Life comes with highs and lows.

We can weather the lows because of Jesus and celebrate the highs because of him, too. And we can remain thankful through it all.

Help your son practice gratitude by thanking God for who he is and what he did by sending Jesus to earth to show us how to live. Circumstances and feelings change from day to day. But Jesus does not. We're thankful because of him. No disclaimers, ifs, ands, or buts. Our thanksgiving is real because of Jesus. Period.

## Biblical Lessons in Action

- How often do you thank God for Jesus? Do you encourage your son to thank God? How can you remember to include this in your prayers more often and to encourage your son to do the same?
- Which Bible story is your favorite? What makes this story special? Have you shared this with your son?
- Does your son have a favorite Bible story? Have you asked him why he likes this story? How often do you talk to your son about Jesus, aside from reading Bible stories to him?
- What's your favorite way to thank God? With audible admissions of thanksgiving? Through song? In service to someone in Jesus' name? With tithes, offerings, or donations?

## Be Grateful for Jesus' Sacrifice

*Thanks be to God for His indescribable gift!* 2 CORINTHIANS 9:15 (BSB)

Our relocation from California to Washington state, compliments of Uncle Sam and my navy career, brought about great sadness with eleven-year-old Jeremy. Previous moves were met with excitement and anticipation, but this time Jeremy struggled with the thought of leaving dear friends behind.

"If Adam and Eve hadn't sinned, then we wouldn't need a military," Jeremy's rant began. "And if we didn't have a military, then Daddy would have a different job. And if Daddy had a different job, we wouldn't be moving."

Technically, Jeremy wasn't wrong, though blaming all his problems on sin was a bit of a stretch. Because of Adam and Eve's original sin, we're all born into sin. We're all sinners and in need of a Savior. From the beginning of time, God knew we would need a Savior, and his plans for Jesus to redeem us from sin weave throughout the entire Bible, from Genesis to Revelation.

Share with your son the significance of Jesus' sacrifice on the cross. Jesus paid a debt he didn't owe to cover our sins and make a way for us to live with God in heaven forever. Allow that realization to encourage an attitude of gratitude in you and your son.

Oh, what great love God has for us that he would send his Son to die on the cross for our sins! Boast on God's love with your son when speaking of Jesus' sacrifice to encourage gratitude and strengthen faith. We have much to be grateful for!

## Biblical Lessons in Action

- Read Mark 15. How does the story of the crucifixion make you feel? Acknowledge the tragedy and sadness of the event and celebrate the joy of Jesus' resurrection. Make sure to thank Jesus in your prayers today for his sacrifice on the cross.
- Consider rereading Bible stories about Jesus over the next several weeks for the purpose of gratitude moments. For example, read the story in John 9 about Jesus healing a blind man. How does this story remind you to be thankful? What about your body or your health can you thank God for?
- How can an attitude of thankfulness for Jesus' sacrifice strengthen your faith walk?
- How can your life reflect a thankful heart to others around you?

## Count Your Blessings

*Give thanks to the LORD for He is good; His loving devotion endures forever.* 1 CHRONICLES 16:34 (BSB)

Even those who don't consider themselves "religious" recognize the benefits of counting blessings. According to studies, a mindset of gratitude releases stress, encourages optimism and positivity, boosts hope, creates a better mood, and increases the ability to face challenges. Some health professionals believe an attitude of gratitude boosts immunities, increases healthier sleep patterns, reduces aches and pains, and lowers blood pressure.

Nurturing a thankful heart in your son nudges him closer to God, because he recognizes everything comes from and belongs to God. All good gifts come from the Heavenly Father who loves us with an incredible, never-ending love. God is good, all the time.

Model gratitude with your son and say "thank you" often. Encourage your son to say thank you. Though it may seem forced in the beginning, he'll internalize the action and initiate the practice on his own soon.

Help your son think beyond the tangible for thanksgiving, too. Help him recognize a beautiful morning, time spent with family, and friendships. Without dwelling too much on the negative, help your son realize even during difficult times he has blessings to be thankful for.

Catch your son being grateful and make a big deal of his actions. Remind him how happy that makes God. Point out the generosity and kindness of others, and help him find ways to be generous and kind, too.

Gratitude takes practice, but it's so worth the effort. A habit of being gracious results in a heart that looks for God's goodness. Help your son count blessings as he walks closer and closer to the Lord.

## Biblical Lessons in Action

- The chorus of an old hymn goes like this: "Count your blessings, name them one by one. Count your blessings, see what God hath done." Try counting your blessings today, naming each one aloud. It's difficult to remember them all, right? Because God is just that good!
- Make a habit of thanking God immediately when something good happens. Found a great parking place? Say, "Thank you, Jesus." Ink pen still works? Say, "Thank you, God."

- Consider keeping a gratitude basket. Place a basket on the table with pens and scraps of paper nearby. Encourage each person in the family to write blessings on the papers and toss them in the basket. Read them aloud at a meal or one evening before bedtime and give thanks.

**PRAYER**

God, you are the giver of good gifts. Thank you for your incredible blessings. Help me be more mindful of my blessings, from the seemingly little blessings to the gigantic ones, too. Cultivate an attitude of gratitude in my heart and help me model and teach that to my son. Amen.

## Remain Faithful during Challenges

*And we know that God works all things together for the good of those who love Him, who are called according to His purpose.* ROMANS 8:28 (BSB)

My long-range military goals included graduate work in the form of a PhD in biology. I'd looked forward to the opportunity and shared the dream with my wife, Julie. When the time came to fill out the application, I pored over the document, dotting every i and crossing every t.

However, the selection board chose another officer with more seniority than me. My emotions ranged from disappointment to discouragement to annoyance, and I'm not sure my internal thoughts were pleasing to God.

Jeremy, only five at the time, shared wise words that eased my grief. "Maybe God has other plans, Daddy." I winked at Julie and said, "Wonder where he's heard that?" She smiled back, and responded, "From his daddy when he didn't get chosen for that part he wanted."

Sometimes it's hard to feel gratitude when life is tough. The Bible doesn't promise an easy life, but God remains good despite difficulties and hardships. Help your son remember that a spirit of gratitude is based on God's goodness, not circumstances or blessings. God promises to bring good out of our difficulties, and it's our job to remain faithful.

Even in dark or hard times, look for bright spots. Lean into God's strength to carry you through and stay in his Word to remember his promises to care for you and never leave you. Pray often and praise him through the challenging times.

Hang on to God and practice gratitude. He's got you. He won't let you down.

# Biblical Lessons in Action

- What's the most challenging situation you've encountered since becoming a parent? Was it hard to feel grateful during that time? How did God get you through that difficulty?
- Think about a family you're close to who's had a tough season in their parenting journey. How did God's faithfulness during that time encourage their faith walk? What "bright spots" were you able to thank him for during that dark season?
- If you're currently experiencing difficult days, do an online search for "Bible verses about strength" and write down several verses on note cards that resonate with your situation. Place the note cards in locations that you'll see them often. Let the verses encourage you and remind you to give thanks, knowing that God is working everything together for your good.

## PRAYER

Dear God, it's hard to feel grateful when times are tough. Remind me that you are always good, regardless of difficult circumstances. Help me feel your presence during hard times. Help me lean into your strength to carry me through and keep me faithful. Thank you for never leaving me. Amen.

# EMBRACE CHRISTIAN LIVING

A CHRIST-CENTERED LIFESTYLE reflects biblical values and enhances spiritual growth. Christianity is about following Christ every single day, and that means living a Christ-centered lifestyle. Our thoughts, words, decisions, actions, work, and play reflect our faith and love for God.

Living for Christ means our life should look different than what we see in the world around us. We clothe ourselves with Christ. Colossians 2:6–7 (NIV) says, "So then, just as you received Christ Jesus as Lord, continue to live your lives in him, rooted and built up in him, strengthened in the faith as you were taught, and over-flowing with thankfulness."

Our priorities change when we become totally devoted to Christ. Rather than self-centered human beings, we strive to be Christ-centered. It's an ongoing process for sure, but you can encourage your son to develop and perfect the character of Christ in his own life on a daily basis.

Some of the areas to help your son align his beliefs and life with the character of Christ are keeping his thoughts positive, choosing healthy relationships, enjoying Christ-centered activities, and identifying God-given talents.

Living out the teachings of Jesus every day takes effort, but as we work toward a Christ-centered life, we can trust God's guidance and presence. He'll lead us in the right direction.

## Keep Your Thoughts Positive

*Finally, brothers and sisters, whatever is true, whatever is noble, whatever is right, whatever is pure, whatever is lovely, whatever is admirable—if anything is excellent or praiseworthy—think about such things.*
PHILIPPIANS 4:8 (NIV)

Do you have that one friend who is always negative and pessimistic? When we lived in Washington state, Jeremy had just such a friend. This eleven-year-old Donald Downer brought down Jeremy's mood each time they hung out. The negativity was palpable when he came home.

When we shared our observations with Jeremy, he bowed just a bit in resistance, but we encouraged him to make every effort to steer conversations toward positivity. Once we pointed out the obvious, Jeremy noticed his friend's pessimism more readily, frequently changed the subject when his friend veered in a negative direction, and we noticed a difference in Jeremy's mood when he came home.

Not every moment of life exudes positivity. Life is tough and challenging. Many moments and days will be unhappy ones. But with the help of the Holy Spirit dwelling in us, we can enjoy the fruit of the Spirit spilling over in our lives and onto those around us. Encourage your son to let these qualities reign: love, joy, peace, patience, kindness, goodness, faithfulness, gentleness, and self-control.

When we clothe ourselves with Christ, joy permeates our life. Joy results from our connection to God and relationship with Jesus. Happiness may be a result of circumstances or happenings, but joy in all circumstances is proof of the Holy Spirit at work in our lives.

Enhance your son's spiritual growth by encouraging him to keep his thoughts positive with whatever is true, noble, right, pure, lovely, admirable, excellent, and praiseworthy.

## Biblical Lessons in Action

- Would you consider yourself an optimist or pessimist? Positive person or negative person? It's easy to think, "Well, that's just my personality. That's how God made me." But, a positive outlook on life, with Christ at the center, is achievable. What practical steps can you take to become a more positive person?
- Think back to a recent conversation with your spouse, a coworker, or a friend that disintegrated quickly into negativity.

How could you have prevented that from happening or steered the conversation in a more positive direction?

- Who do you know who exudes positivity and joy? Do others seem to gravitate toward that person? What do you find most attractive about that person's words and actions?
- How does knowing Christ bring you joy?

## PRAYER

Dear God, thank you for the joy that comes from knowing Christ as my Savior. Please help my life reflect the joy of Jesus through my positive thoughts, words, and actions. Help me "think on these things" from Philippians 4:8 and may they always bring a smile to my face. Amen.

## Choose Healthy Relationships

*As iron sharpens iron, so one man sharpens another.* PROVERBS 27:17 (BSB)

God designed his children for relationships. The most desired relationship of all, obviously, is our connection to God. Through Jesus Christ, we can have a personal relationship with our Heavenly Father. The Bible uses "family" and "friend" when speaking of our relationship with God, expressing the essence of the kind of relationship God wants with us.

From the early Bible stories of Adam and Eve and throughout the rest of the Bible, God's Word reveals his desire for relationships and his instructions on making them work best. Yet even with his guidelines, relationships are complicated.

To best strengthen our faith and grow our relationship with the Lord, choosing healthy relationships is essential for a Christ-centered lifestyle that is pleasing to God.

Nine-year-old Jeb Daniel and a neighbor friend liked playing video games together. After an afternoon at Sam's house, Jeb Daniel reluctantly admitted to us that the new games Sam chose disturbed him. When we researched, we found them to be too violent for kids their age. Jeb Daniel bravely told Sam his thoughts about the games. Their friendship fizzled after that, but it was a wise choice, in our opinion.

God wants us to experience relationships that reflect him, ones that emulate Christ. Your son may have to make hard decisions about friendships as he matures in his relationship with Christ. Though we're not advocating dumping a friendship for small infractions, we think it's important to help your son choose relationships where he'll sharpen others and be sharpened in return.

# Biblical Lessons in Action

- Do you have any unhealthy relationships or friendships? Perfect relationships are modeled in the Trinity—God the Father, God the Son, and God the Holy Spirit. If you currently have a relationship that isn't furthering your walk with the Lord and strengthening your faith, consider reevaluating the relationship and making changes.
- How can you help your son choose friendships wisely without becoming a "helicopter parent"?
- What qualities do you look for in a friend? What qualities do you exhibit that make you a desirable friend? How can you help your son look for Christlike qualities in friends?
- What long-standing friendships do you treasure? What do you think kept those friendships vibrant and solid? Have you thanked that person recently for being part of your life?

## PRAYER

Dear God, relationships are hard on this side of heaven. Help me choose the kinds of relationships and friendships that would be pleasing to you and further my spiritual journey. Help me model right relationships for my son. Bless the relationships he has now and the ones in his future. Amen.

# Enjoy Christ-Centered Activities

*Do not be conformed to this world, but be transformed by the renewal of your mind, that by testing you may discern what is the will of God, what is good and acceptable and perfect.* ROMANS 12:2 (ESV)

During middle school, Jeb Daniel gave up baseball. You see, the only way to excel as a homeschooled student who played baseball in our county was to join a traveling ball team. The problem with traveling teams? Understandably, tournaments took place out of town for entire weekends. "I don't want to miss church for the whole season," Jeb Daniel said.

Much later, Jeb Daniel began to play disc golf. Over the years, he's won several tournaments and continues to improve his game as a young adult. He doesn't regret giving up baseball, and he found a way to continue his love of outdoor sports.

Some people think Christians lead unexciting, dull lives. Though much of what the world deems "fun" doesn't line up with a Christian lifestyle, walking with Christ is anything but boring. We're called to be in this world but not of it, but that doesn't mean we check out from life on earth! Our lives should be marked with an anticipation and hope for a future with Christ in heaven, and God gives us a world of fun things that boast of his goodness and grace until that time arrives. Help your son choose activities that glorify and honor God and point others to Jesus along the way.

Whether those activities are directly related to Christian friends and church fellowship or surrounded by God's children elsewhere, Christ-centered activities build our faith and strengthen our walk with God.

## Biblical Lessons in Action

- What activities fill your family's calendar? How can you make sure others see Christ in you with each of those commitments?
- Are there some activities that your family takes part in that might not be pleasing to God or take time away from God? How can you make changes that will better fit the spiritual needs of your family?
- What was your favorite extracurricular activity as a child? Does your son enjoy that activity too? How can you involve your son in some of your passions and activities and vice versa?
- Think back to a recent activity that your family enjoyed taking part in. How did you see Jesus in others around you? How did you let Jesus' light shine in your words and actions?

## PRAYER

God, just as David went "leaping and dancing before the Lord" in 2 Samuel 6:16, help my joy for Jesus show in my work and play. Help me initiate and enjoy Christ-centered activities that build my faith and encourage my son's. Help me keep you at the center of all I do. Amen.

# Identify God-Given Talents

*Every good and perfect gift is from above, coming down from the Father of the heavenly lights, who does not change like shifting shadows.* JAMES 1:17 (NIV)

That same son who seemed to have a propensity toward sports activities also had an interest in guitar. Jeb Daniel didn't enjoy singing in front of others, so this came as a surprise to us.

Jeb Daniel faithfully took lessons with the guitar we gifted him for his birthday. It didn't take long for his talent to shine, and he spent his middle school and high school years playing guitar with the youth praise band. He also served as an intern with the college ministry praise team and played during some worship services as a young adult. He enjoyed using his gifts and talents, given to him by God, to glorify the Lord.

Spiritual gifts are special abilities and talents given to Christians by the Holy Spirit for the purpose of serving God and others, and a quick search for those gifts shows where they are listed in specific verses in Romans, 1 Corinthians, and Ephesians. Every believer receives a spiritual gift or gifts when they receive the gift of salvation.

Not to be confused with natural talents and capabilities, like baseball prowess or musical inclinations, also given to us by God for his purposes, spiritual gifts include such abilities as prophecy, encouragement, leadership, wisdom, and many others. Help your son understand spiritual gifts, but don't be surprised if his gift isn't evident until later in his faith walk. In the meantime, build on the natural gifts, talents, and abilities given to your son by God, and help him find ways to glorify God.

## Biblical Lessons in Action

- Do an online search for "biblical spiritual gifts." Also read about them in Romans 12:6–8, 1 Corinthians 12:8–10, and 1 Corinthians 12:28–30. What spiritual gift have you identified in yourself?
- How do you use your spiritual gift to serve God? In what ways do you serve others with your spiritual gift? Ponder a recent opportunity to use your spiritual gift to serve someone in your extended family, church, or community.
- What natural ability do you possess? Are you a good cook, math whiz, or talented artist? How do you use that ability to serve God? To serve others? How can you model this to your son?
- In what ways can you remind your son that God made him for a special purpose?

### PRAYER

Dear God, thank you for creating me with the unique talents, abilities, and spiritual gifts you ordained just for me. Help me use each one for your glory, to serve you and others. Help me guide my son to find his special gifts and use them lavishly for your glory, too. Amen.

# SERVE GOD AND OTHERS

JESUS MODELED A life of selfless service that is an example for you and your son to follow. He set the ultimate example of what it means to serve God and others. Through his life, death, and resurrection, Jesus showed us exactly how we should live. Striving to live like Jesus and serving God with our actions and God-given finances deepens our trust in God and strengthens our faith walk.

God calls us to serve. The Bible says in 1 John 3:18 (NLT), "Dear children, let's not merely say that we love each other; let us show the truth by our actions." Loving others, as God requires from his Word, means serving them. We live out our faith when we serve God, serve family, serve the church, and serve others. Investing in our community and the world around us, done in Jesus' name, points people toward God.

Like previously mentioned principles, it's never too early nor too late to model service with your son. Even if he's still an infant, make a habit of serving others. By the time he's old enough to recognize the act of serving others, you'll be such a natural at doing so he'll recognize the joy and satisfaction you receive from answering God's call to serve, and he will desire to serve, too.

## Serve God

*Only fear the* LORD *and serve him faithfully with all your heart. For consider what great things he has done for you.* 1 SAMUEL 12:24 (ESV)

God created us, saved us, and has plans for us to live in heaven with him forever. That's reason enough right there to want to serve him our entire lives! When we consider what great things God has done for us, and does for us every day, our hearts should swell with such gratitude that we desire to serve him wholeheartedly, with joy and thanksgiving.

Jesus reminds us often that he came to serve. If we want to emulate Christ—and we do—then we should strive to serve others daily. We often get so busy with "life" that we fail to notice others' needs. It will take some effort and intentionality to recognize opportunities to serve. Serving means giving of ourselves to meet the needs of another person. It's a lifestyle of putting others first.

Help your son recognize many ways to serve God. First and foremost, point out to your son that obeying his parents is an act of serving God. Following God's commands in Scripture strengthens his relationship with the Lord, builds his trust in God's faithfulness, and opens the door to a deeper faith. Your son can serve God by following his instructions in the Bible on the right way to live a life that is pleasing to God.

On a deeper level, serving others, those created in the image of God, ultimately means serving God. Reflect the love of God by serving others. Serving him is serving others—serving others is serving him.

## Biblical Lessons in Action

- What are you most thankful for regarding your relationship with God? How can you find a tangible way to express your gratitude to him? How can you share those with your son?
- How is serving others a direct reflection of your love for God? What service opportunities can you take part in with your son?
- What aspects of Jesus' ministry and time on earth do you want to emulate most? What qualities of Jesus do you excel in and which ones could use more work? What practical things can you do today or this week to work on those qualities?

## PRAYER

Dear God, thank you for Jesus' example of a life of service. Help me have a heart to serve you and those you love. Show me ways I can serve others every day. Help me not get so busy with my own life that I miss opportunities to serve others around me. Amen.

## Serve Family

*As each has received a gift, use it to serve one another, as good stewards of God's varied grace.* 1 PETER 4:10 (ESV)

One of my husband's special abilities is teaching, especially imparting wisdom about nature. He delighted in serving his family by teaching our homeschooled crew to love God's creation. David's even helped me gain an appreciation for certain creepy critters and their beauty, though he hasn't quite taken away some of my fears of said creatures!

My love language to my family is giving gifts and treats. Not expensive ones but thoughtful ones, like a favorite fountain drink or candy bar or new pair of fun socks. I especially love baking treats I know my family loves. My children enjoyed sharing my baking talents with their friends. Church friends, youth ministers, piano teachers, dance instructors, and others came to love and somewhat expect treats from us. By serving my family, I inadvertently served their friends as well.

Serving our family should be our primary ministry. God blessed us with the people in our home. He very deliberately placed us with the ones he chose to be our family, and he called us to love and serve those in our family.

Serving family means putting them first. Help your son learn to help out at home and do chores joyfully. Model taking care of family members' needs, showing compassion, speaking kindly, sharing, prioritizing time spent together, celebrating accomplishments, and loving well in other ways, too.

Be grateful for your family and thank God often for them. Find ways every day to serve your family, with a smile on your face and joy in your heart.

## Biblical Lessons in Action

- What's your favorite way to serve your family? In what ways does your son serve his family? Model an attitude of gratitude by remembering to thank other family members often for ways they serve the family.
- How can you be your son's biggest cheerleader? Make a list of ways you can encourage, support, and serve him.
- Do an online search for "families in the Bible." Plan to read different Bible stories about family over the next several weeks. Each time you read, think about what family members did well to serve their family. Pay attention to where they failed and what went wrong.

## Serve the Church

*Therefore, whenever we have the opportunity, we should do good to everyone—especially to those in the family of faith.* GALATIANS 6:10 (NLT)

While living in Virginia, our older children began a barrage of begging for new toys with each trip to the store. Though most of the toys they asked for weren't outrageously expensive, Jeremy seemed to always want a new dinosaur figurine, another sea creature toy, or a different fast-moving race car. I decided it was time for a lesson on budgeting and finances.

When Jeremy received a monetary treat in the mail from Mema, I sat down with him at the table and placed four envelopes in front of him. We talked about divvying out the total amount in four ways: money for tithe, a percentage to save, a certain amount to spend serving someone else, and a small amount to spend now.

Jeremy put the bills and coins in the appropriate envelopes and arranged them in a square, two on top and two on bottom. He let his seven-year-old finger trace the space in the middle, from top to bottom and left to right, and said, "Look, Mommy. A cross."

While I was focused on the envelopes themselves, Jeremy visualized deeper. And, yes, Jeremy—it's all about the cross!

We can show our appreciation for what Jesus did on the cross by serving those in our church body. Great examples of church service include helping in the nursery, teaching a youth or college class, serving in men's or women's ministry, cleaning the church kitchen, restocking the church pantry, mowing the lawn, sweeping the floors of the fellowship hall, and more.

Look to the cross and serve him.

## Biblical Lessons in Action

- In what different ministries within your church have you served? What's your favorite way to serve at church? Does your church often lack volunteers? How can you encourage others to step up and serve?
- What motivates you to want to serve in your church?
- How can your service be an example to your son? Given your son's age, how can the two of you serve together?
- Are there certain people or families that are members of your church that stand out as true servants of God? Why do you think they prioritize that service?

## Serve Others

*"The King will reply, 'Truly I tell you, whatever you did for one of the least of these brothers and sisters of mine, you did for me.'"* MATTHEW 25:40 (NIV)

I felt strongly about teaching my children to serve others, but with a recent move, boxes to unpack, a one-year-old, four-year-old, and seven-year-old to care for and homeschool, and a husband in school full-time for navy training, I'll admit sometimes I served out of self-imposed obligation.

I enlisted the kids' help in baking cookies for a nearby homeless shelter. With cookies in hand, we waited while a shelter employee settled a young couple with a toddler. The father hoisted two large garbage bags of belongings. Suddenly, my heart warmed to think of the toddler nibbling on our cookies, and my joy of serving God's children resurfaced.

When our motivation to serve comes from a deep love for God, we will naturally want to serve others around us. Help your son understand that serving others can mean a deliberate and intentional action, like volunteering at a soup kitchen or delivering cookies to a homeless shelter.

But it can also mean a lifestyle that reflects God's love in every facet of your son's day—doing chores to help the family, assisting a classmate with books, helping a teacher clean desks, holding a door open for strangers, giving up your seat on the bus, donating clothes to a boys' facility, volunteering with a church ministry regularly, and so much more.

Jesus modeled a life of selfless service every day. He made the ultimate sacrifice when he died on the cross for us. Following his example of serving God's children is the least we can do in appreciation.

## Biblical Lessons in Action

- As a family, how can you serve your community? If you already have a place you serve regularly, who else can you invite to serve along with you? If you haven't yet found a place to serve, what's holding you back?
- Have you ever been on the receiving end of someone's act of service? How did it make you feel? How can you pay that act forward and include your son?

- How can you teach your son to recognize the needs of others? Does your compassion for others shine boldly enough for your son to see?
- How does loving God encourage you to serve? How can service to others strengthen your faith walk? Who will you serve today?

## PRAYER

Dear God, help me model Jesus' life of selfless service and serve those around me. Help me serve joyfully and lavishly. Help me be mindful of the needs of others and never turn my back on one of your children. Grow my son's compassion each day to serve you more, too. Amen.

# SET BEHAVIORAL BOUNDARIES

SETTING BOUNDARIES TO govern your son's actions teaches responsible behavior and guides him toward making good and right choices. Boundaries serve as teaching tools to shape character and promote positive behavior. Setting boundaries is less about imposing restrictions and more about nurturing healthy relationships, safeguarding your son, and respecting those he encounters.

Help your son understand that he needs limits and boundaries to keep him and others around him safe. With age-appropriate conversations, help your child recognize that limits and boundaries provide a sense of security and a guardrail for what is right and wrong according to God's standards. Remind him of this verse in Proverbs 1:8 (NIV): "Listen, my son, to your father's instruction and do not forsake your mother's teaching."

When your son pushes past boundaries and disobeys, the consequences you enforce help him learn responsible behavior. Consequences of disobedience, administered with love and explanations, serve to teach your son and correct unwanted behavior.

To teach responsible behavior, discipline in love, hold your son accountable, be consistent with limitations and consequences, and praise good conduct. Help your son recognize God's admonitions for right behavior in relation to the boundaries you set and remind him often of God's never-ending love.

## Discipline in Love

*My son, do not despise the LORD's discipline, and do not resent his rebuke, because the LORD disciplines those he loves, as a father the son he delights in.* PROVERBS 3:11–12 (NIV)

Becka and Dean's preteen son, Dax, said cruel words to Sloan at a youth event. Dax enjoyed getting a laugh out of other kids, including our son. Becka felt comfortable confiding in me, since our son took part in the infraction.

Becka took away screen privileges and said, "Dax, I'm sure you realize what you did was wrong. Your unkind words hurt Sloan. We'll talk about this tomorrow and discuss the consequences of your behavior then."

Becka recognized emotions clouded her judgment at that moment and might affect her word choices with Dax.

The following day, Becka, Dean, and Dax talked. With time to cool off, Becka pointed out Dax's wrongdoing, reminding him of Jesus' admonition to treat others as they wanted to be treated. And with time to dwell on his unkind words, Dax admitted he owed Sloan an apology. He accepted his punishment of no screen privileges for two days and crafted an apology note. My husband and I had a similar conversation with our son, and he, too, prepared an apology note and lost video game privileges.

God disciplines because he loves us. He delights in us. He wants what is best for us. God disciplines us to guide our steps and to correct our behavior for our own good.

The root word of "discipline" is "disciple." One of our biggest roles as parents is to train our sons to be disciples of Jesus. Our discipline, always meted out in love, serves to guide and correct our sons, those children in whom we delight!

## Biblical Lessons in Action

- God disciplines for correction and guidance because he loves us. Discuss with your parenting partner or a trusted mentor practical disciplinary actions that mirror God's love.
- Reflect on a time in your childhood when you felt unfairly punished. Use that situation to discuss that we don't always give or receive discipline perfectly. Ask your son how you can do better with discipline in the future.
- Counselors and teachers encourage kids to control their anger in different ways, like counting to ten or taking a deep breath.

With your partner or a trusted mentor, list five ways to curb anger when behavior issues arise in the future to help you discipline for correction rather than punishment.

- How can you show love to your son in the midst of a reprimand? What words can express love despite high tensions?

## Hold Him Accountable

*So then, each of us will give an account of ourselves to God.* ROMANS 14:12 (NIV)

Afraid of water and not a strong swimmer, eight-year-old Jeb Daniel hated water activities. Perhaps, then, it shouldn't have surprised me –but it did—when I realized he was skipping hair washing at night. You'd think I would've noticed his still-sweaty, matted hair the day after a shower, but, well, this busy mom of four just didn't clue in.

It finally dawned on me the shampoo bottle never moved, and his hair was filthy. He explained his fear of sticking his head under the shower water, and we made other suggestions for cleanliness. However, Jeb Daniel lost coveted playtime with his older brother for lying to David and me.

God's Word says we'll be held accountable for our actions. Help your son recognize that in addition to disobeying God, his sins have the potential to disrespect and harm others.

One way you can encourage accountability in your son is to model your own accountability. When you mess up, admit your failure and accept the consequences. If you miss a deadline at work, don't make excuses or lie about the situation. Own up to your shortcomings and do whatever it takes to make it right.

Help your son realize he can learn from his mistakes. If he gets a bad grade for missed homework, let that serve as encouragement to complete his work on time. Following through on the consequences you've established for wrong behavior also helps your son's accountability.

When your son learns accountability for his actions, he moves farther along the path to responsible behavior.

## Biblical Lessons in Action

- How have you shown accountability to your son? How do your daily actions serve as an example to your son?
- What helps hold you accountable when "no one is watching"? What helps you remember that God sees all and knows all, even when you think you've gotten away with your sin?
- Is there a shortcoming you struggle with? Is there a sin you're having trouble repenting of? Have you considered asking a godly friend to hold you accountable for that action?
- Are you quick to apologize to your son when you make a mistake? Or do you make excuses for your actions? How can you change that?

## PRAYER

Dear God, forgive me of my sins. Help me always recognize right from wrong and help me make right decisions that please you. Keep me accountable for my actions, even when I think no one is watching. Instill in my son the desire and accountability to be obedient to you. Amen.

# Be Consistent

*Know then in your heart that as a man disciplines his son, so the LORD your God disciplines you. Observe the commands of the LORD your God, walking in obedience to him and revering him.* DEUTERONOMY 8:5–6 (NIV)

Kids are quick to call us parents on discrepancies, especially when it relates to a sibling, right? "But you let Jeb Daniel have extra time to finish his schoolwork, Mommy," Jeremy said when I threatened to take away outside time because of an incomplete assignment. He was right, and we discussed how to solve the problem together.

Our sons need consistent boundaries and consequences. Consistency helps establish structure in our home and beyond and lets your son know exactly what consequences to expect with infractions. Consistency helps your son stay within the set boundaries and limits. However, don't confuse inconsistency with new, age-appropriate boundaries and consequences as your son grows from a preschooler to a teenager. Consistency also doesn't mean you throw flexibility or mercy out the window. Model God's grace and mercy with your son if a situation warrants it and explain your actions accordingly.

Discuss both rules and consequences in depth with your son and stay consistent with your responses. These expectations give your son a clear understanding of what to expect in different situations. And what you expect of him.

Share God's consistency with your son. The Bible says God is the same yesterday, today, and forever. His Word reminds us God is unchanging. That is a consistency we can depend on. Which means his love for us is unchanging and will remain the same. He will never ever leave us nor forsake us. That's a consistency worth celebrating!

## Biblical Lessons in Action

- Do you struggle to be consistent with rules and boundaries with your son? Why do you think that happens? How can you make sure your consistency is not affected by ever-changing moods, stressful situations, or other outside influences?
- Were you raised with inconsistent boundaries and consequences? How can you break that generational stronghold to be consistent with your son?
- Do you encourage your son's input on consequences and disciplinary actions? How can you have a conversation with your son about boundaries while maintaining the control expected of you as the parent?
- Consider making a list of God's qualities that are immutable. Talk about the list with your son. With your son, give thanks for his unchanging love, grace, and mercy.

## Praise Good Conduct

*Kind words are like honey—sweet to the soul and healthy for the body.*
PROVERBS 16:24 (NLT)

Praising your son's behavior is an excellent tool to encourage good behavior. Who doesn't like to be praised and affirmed? "Catch your son doing good," as they say, and reward that behavior with sweet words—a balm to the soul, healthy for the body, and as tasty as honey.

Sometimes it's easy to let good behavior go unnoticed. When your son behaves the way you expect him to, try not to miss an opportunity to strengthen that good behavior and impress upon him the desire to keep up the good work. Positive and immediate reinforcement instills the motivation to obey and stay within set boundaries.

Here are a few tips for making praise an effective discipline tool.

- Offer specific praise when your son is doing good. Instead of saying, "Great job," when your son cleans his room, offer these words: "Wow, I really like how you put everything in its place. I love how you cleaned your room on your own. That's such a great help to Mom and Dad."
- Point out and praise your son's effort, not just the end result. Praising his effort helps him continue to try his best. Try to offer positive reinforcement immediately when your son does something good or stays within the boundaries. Praising him later at a meal or before bedtime works great, but rewarding him with your words immediately is even sweeter!

Generally, your son wants to please you and excel. And he treasures attention from you when that happens.

## Biblical Lessons in Action

- How do you feel when someone gives you an accolade or praise? What's your favorite way to be praised? Do you enjoy words, physical touch, or a special treat? Do you know which method your son prefers most?
- How can you be more attentive to "catch your son doing good"? What can you do today that will help you be more observant to notice your son's good behavior?

- Make a list of *attaboys* to share with your son. Get creative and personal with the words you want to say. Plan to share those words at appropriate moments.
- What words of praise can you offer to God today to express your gratitude for his never-ending love? Who else can you praise with your words today?

## PRAYER

Dear God, you are holy and perfect and good and worthy of all my praise. I know you delight in my praise. Help me remember to use words of praise with my son, to grow his relationship with you, strengthen his faith, and encourage responsible behavior. I love you, Lord. Amen.

# PARENTING PRINCIPLE 8 | LEAD BY EXAMPLE

BECAUSE YOUR SON will imitate your actions and reactions as he encounters life situations, lead well to provide a godly example. Our sons watch us more often than we realize. Sometimes, it may be a quick glance or momentary observation. Other times, our sons may scrutinize our actions and reactions, pondering our motivation or reason behind our behavior. As parents responsible for pointing our sons to Jesus Christ to build their faith and character, we want those observations to serve as teachable moments and be positive and impactful. We need to be intentional to lead by example with our sons to further their walk with the Lord.

First Corinthians 16:13 (NIV) says, "Be on your guard; stand firm in the faith; be courageous; be strong." When you follow these directives, you model doing what's right in any situation to your son and stamp that character trait on his heart.

You can lead by example first and foremost by guarding your heart. Letting your son see you guard your actions and language is the outward expression of guarding your heart. Treating others like Christ would is a crucial example to your son, also. When you love and respect your spouse or partner, you not only encourage your son's future behavior, you teach them how Jesus wants us to treat all of God's children.

## Guard Your Heart

*Above all else, guard your heart, for everything you do flows from it.*
PROVERBS 4:23 (NIV)

My four-year-old grandson and I tagged along one afternoon when my sons and hubby played disc golf. Benaiah stopped to pick some weeds and handed them to me, announcing, "Because you're my heart."

Well, as you can imagine, his words melted this Grandmommy's heart, causing the spillover to leak from the corners of my eyes.

The heart. Perhaps the most important organ of our body. God created our hearts to be the very center of our being. Our heart controls our emotions and feelings, our thoughts and desires, and our actions and reactions. In other words, our heart is our source of life. To guard our heart means to protect it from the negativity and grime of the world and to fill it with God—his words from Scripture, his goodness, and his character.

Let your son see you filling your heart with God. Read Scripture with him, but also let him see you reading God's Word often. Listen to music that's pleasing to God. Watch shows and other forms of media acceptable in God's eyes. Surround yourself with Christian friends. Avoid places and situations rife with temptation. (However, the authors of this book aren't implying we should live in a bubble, removed from serving the world in God's name.) Saturate your life with God and his goodness to guard your heart.

We are God's heart, the apple of his eye, and he expects us to lead our sons to Christ through our example of guarding our heart daily.

## Biblical Lessons in Action

- What can you do daily to keep your heart clean and undefiled? Are there practices and habits you need to eliminate or change? Places and people you should avoid or limit exposure to?
- How are you actively stamping God's Word on your heart? How can you filter every action and reaction through what God's Word says?
- Guarding our heart is a difficult task when attempted on our own; we can only do so with God's strength. What is your favorite verse about God's strength? With your son, do an online search to find a powerful verse about strength for both of you to memorize this week.

- How can you purposefully show your son what you do to guard your heart? How can you teach him to guard his heart at home, school, and play?

## Guard Your Actions and Language

*Keep your mouth free of perversity; keep corrupt talk far from your lips.*
PROVERBS 4:24 (NIV)

One grandson loves to call owls when he comes for a visit. When Benaiah was just three years old, David used an owl call in our backyard, and in minutes, two barred owls flew to the top of a pine tree, a cacophony of calls erupting. "Let me do it," Benaiah said, reaching for the call. Benaiah mimicked David perfectly, blowing air through the plastic device to result in a "who-who who-whooooo" worthy of an owl's ear.

When Benaiah handed the call back to David, my husband smiled at me, wiped grandson-spit off the instrument, and called again. Well, as you can probably imagine, the next time Benaiah took a turn, he mimicked David's actions again. This time to include wiping the device on his shirt, just like Granddaddy. He had no idea why that was part of the process to call owls, but he wanted to get it just right.

Our sons (and grandsons) watch closely what we do and listen intently to what we say. We want our actions, reactions, and language to reflect godliness. When our sons mimic us, let's hope we like what we see—and God does, too!

Pour Scripture into your heart and your son's heart at every opportunity, to draw closer to Jesus. Let every action and reaction be a direct reflection of your love for Jesus and God's love for you. Filter your thoughts, and in turn, your words, through God's Word.

Guard your actions and language and teach your son to do the same.

## Biblical Lessons in Action

- How can you filter your thoughts through the truth of God's Word to ensure godly actions and reactions? When you falter, how can you make it right with God and those affected by your actions?
- How does filling your mind and heart with God's Word help you control the words that come out of your mouth?

- Are you actively striving to speak positive, uplifting words to others? How can you refrain from negativity or unkindness in your words and responses? How can you use your efforts as a way to teach your son to do the same thing?
- Obviously, no parent is perfect. We all make mistakes. Can you recall a recent time your son saw you behave or speak in an ungodly way? How did you use that as a teachable moment to help your son learn to guard his actions and language?

## PRAYER

Dear God, forgive me when my actions and language are displeasing to you. Reveal behavior that doesn't line up with your Word. Allow the Holy Spirit to convict me and give me a desire to make it right quickly. Let me be a godly example with my words and actions. Amen.

## Treat Others Like Christ Would

*Be kind and compassionate to one another, forgiving each other, just as in Christ God forgave you.* EPHESIANS 4:32 (NIV)

Sometimes I got it right as a parent.

While running errands with my boys, I stared at the blinking lights and laughed out loud. "What's funny, Mommy?" Jeb Daniel asked.

"Well, I just silently prayed for that mailman up ahead. I thought it was an emergency response vehicle." I'll admit I was proud of teaching my kids to pray for emergency situations we encountered.

"That's okay, Mommy. He must've needed prayer today."

Often, I got it wrong as a parent.

I took the kids to the library to refresh our stack of books. When Jeremy moved a beanbag in the kids' section, the librarian bolted from her office and scolded him. This mama bear reacted unkindly and proceeded to scold her. Jeremy was more hurt by my reaction than by the insensitive librarian's words to him. Even though I thought her harshness was unmerited, I shouldn't have treated her the way I did. At home, I made a phone call to the librarian and apologized.

One of the greatest services you can offer your son is to teach him to treat people the way Christ did. To love them unconditionally, despite their differences and shortcomings, regardless of how they treat us. To be kind, respectful, gentle, and loving. To be willing to stand up to injustice and cruelty. To allow the Holy Spirit to help us point them to Jesus.

Treating others like Christ would reminds us and those around us of God's great love. It's all about him!

## Biblical Lessons in Action

- How do you react to the Holy Spirit's conviction when you miss the mark? Are you defiant or humble? Do you fix the situation or attempt to ignore it? What can you do to be more aware of the Holy Spirit's prompting?
- Talk with your son about someone you know who best demonstrates Christlike treatment of others. How might you and your son emulate that person's godliness?
- You've heard it before, but it's worth repeating. Love is more than just a feeling—love is an action. How do your actions show the love of Christ to your son and those around you?
- When you or your son encounter someone who is different than you, does your response reflect the love of Jesus? If not, what can you do to change that reaction?

### PRAYER

God, please help me value and love people the way you do. Impress upon me ways to live in harmony with your children. Help me love the outcasts and sinners, because after all, when I look in a mirror, that's me. Help me treat others with love and respect, just like Jesus. Amen.

# Love and Respect Your Spouse

*However, each one of you also must love his wife as he loves himself, and the wife must respect her husband.* EPHESIANS 5:33 (NIV)

At a church luncheon, one of my wife's friends joined us at our family table. When the conversation turned to my early-morning commute and my wife's homeschooling responsibilities, Julie's friend said in jest, "You mean Julie doesn't get up with you every morning and cook breakfast before you leave?" Just to be humorous, I rolled my eyes and said, "Not hardly."

I saw the dejected look on my wife's face, and apparently, so did Jeb Daniel. He quickly quipped, "But Mommy makes sure he takes homemade muffins or sausage casserole to work every day for breakfast." Thankful for his answer, I could've said instead, "I rise early, but Julie stays up late every night writing lesson plans or preparing my breakfast for the next day." Or even the most honest answer: "I don't like eating breakfast first thing, so Julie graciously prepares food for me to eat later at work."

But I didn't. And, I apologized to her and our sons later.

One of the greatest gifts we can give our children to help them with familial relationships is to love well those closest to us, but especially our spouse. For some families, that may mean treating a former spouse with loving kindness and respect, too. When your son sees evidence of Christ in you through your words and actions toward those closest to you, he'll see a resemblance to the Lord's goodness, kindness, grace, mercy, and love, and he'll be more apt to extend that treatment to those around him.

Strong and loving family relationships help your son feel safe, secure, and loved.

## Biblical Lessons in Action

- How do strong relationships with those closest to you provide an atmosphere for your son to thrive? How can that faithful stability help your son feel loved and secure?
- Did you grow up in a home with parents who exhibited a loving marriage? What about that relationship do you want to replicate, and what do you want to change?
- How do you show love and respect to those closest to you? How can those actions strengthen the community of people that helps you raise your son?
- How do your actions show those closest to you that you value them? How can you teach your son to value and respect family relationships?

## PRAYER

Dear God, thank you for the network of people who help me raise my son. Thank you for picking out just the right community for me. You knew who I'd need to raise my son best. Help me love and respect those closest to me in everything I do and say. Amen.

# ENCOURAGE HIGH MORAL STANDARDS

GOD'S STANDARD FOR what is moral and good is high, but attainable with his help. Though the world's version of right and wrong often differs from God's view, most would agree high moral standards include such values as loyalty, trustworthiness, empathy, respect, fairness, and responsibility.

God's admonitions help us choose right from wrong, because he wants us to "sin no more" and live like Jesus. God also knows we need high moral standards to live in harmony with others, whether that's our own families, the community where we live, or the world around us. High moral standards help us choose behaviors considered acceptable and right by society to make the world a better place in which to live.

Encouraging your son to reach for high moral standards, like responsibility, respectfulness, trustworthiness, and fairness, nurtures his character and strengthens his faith in the one who mandates those standards, our Heavenly Father, and the one who came to live out perfect morality as an example to follow, Jesus Christ.

Remind your son of the Bible verse that teaches he's never too young to set an example. First Timothy 4:12 (NIV) says, "Don't let anyone look down on you because you are young, but set an example for the believers in speech, in conduct, in love, in faith and in purity."

## Responsibility

*So whoever knows the right thing to do and fails to do it, for him it is sin.*
JAMES 4:17 (ESV)

A responsible person holds himself accountable for his actions. One who is responsible can be trusted to do what is right and good and expected.

As a twelve-year-old, the oldest kid in the neighborhood group that included his siblings, Jeremy was often the leader of creative games and adventures in the small patch of trees and sagebrush behind our new house. Unbeknownst to us, some of the kids were hiding from their parents and smoking cigarettes in the woods, too.

Jeremy's feelings of responsibility for his younger brother and sisters took precedence over impressing new neighbors, and we were pleased that he shared this information with us out of concern for all involved.

Even knowing that it might turn his friends against him, Jeremy made the responsible decision to let us know. Parents were appreciative, kids were forgiving, and Jeremy earned the admiration of the younger kids even more.

A strong faith in God and a commitment to his mandates applied to everyday life situations helps us act responsibly. Encourage your son to be accountable for his actions, to follow rules, and to fulfill his moral obligations to those around him.

To encourage accountability for actions and obligations with your son, start by giving age-appropriate household chores and tasks. Help him recognize his role as a contributing member of the family, and in turn, of the world around him. Teach decision-making skills and discuss learning from mistakes. Praise often and capitalize on teachable moments to point your son to Jesus and encourage high morals.

## Biblical Lessons in Action

- Think back to your preteen or teenage years. Who was the most responsible person in your friend group? How did that person act or behave differently from their peers to earn that recognition from you?
- How can you model responsibility to your son? What specific behavior did you demonstrate today that reflected responsible character? What other responsible adults are role models for

your son? Have you thanked them for their influence on your son's life?

- What household responsibilities have you given your son? How do you hold him accountable for those responsibilities? How can you train him to hold himself accountable?
- Read some of the stories about Jesus in one of the Gospels. How did he demonstrate responsibility in his actions in each story?

## PRAYER

Dear God, hold me accountable for my actions. Help me choose what's right and good according to the Bible, not the world's standards. Remind me to help my son grow into a young man of character, one who behaves responsibly and one who takes responsibility for the needy like Jesus did. Amen.

## Respectfulness

*Show yourself in all respects to be a model of good works, and in your teaching show integrity, dignity, and sound speech that cannot be condemned.* TITUS 2:7-8A (ESV)

Four-year-old Jeremy's first experience with a homeless individual happened on a visit to California. I noticed Jeremy's eyes fixed on a gentleman sleeping on a concrete bench at the park. Tattered clothes, matted hair, and no coat for the cold caught Jeremy's attention. I tried to explain delicately. "Sometimes people have needs that are bigger than they can handle, and they have no one to take care of them."

"But doesn't he have a mommy?" Jeremy asked.

Tears pricked my eyes. As much as I liked knowing my son thought a mommy could solve any problem, my heart hurt with the realization that this man and many others lacked someone with a heart as big as a mommy or daddy to care for them.

When we finished our time at the playground, we stopped by a fast-food place and bought gift cards to give away.

Teaching your son to be respectful of others, regardless of differences like economic status, skin color, age, physical appearance, political stance, religious background, or ethnicity, encourages him to have the empathy and love for others that Jesus did.

Respect starts in the home. Teach your son to respect each family member and establish consequences for disrespect, like removal of privileges or a toy for a limited time. Praise and reward respectfulness. And most importantly, model respect to others for your son to see—the cashier, the restaurant server, the beggar on the street corner, the child next door, or the owner of a business. Respectfulness reflects good character.

# Biblical Lessons in Action

- What can you do every day to show respect to your spouse? Son? Extended family member? Coworker? Someone you meet for the first time?
- What are some words and actions that demonstrate respect? In opposition, what words and actions display disrespect?
- When someone disrespects you, what is your typical first reaction? Do you feel that response shows Christ to the other party or to your son, who might be watching? How could you handle your reaction differently next time?
- Did your parents show respect to one another? To you and others? If your parents modeled respect, how can you perpetuate that quality to a greater degree in your own relationships? If your parents lacked respectfulness, what can you do to end the cycle of disrespect?

## PRAYER

Dear God, you're the creator of the world—everything belongs to you. Teach me to respect what's yours, from human beings to nature to the world around me. Help me embrace your children with love and respect, whether our differences are small or huge. Help me love like Jesus. Amen.

# Trustworthiness

*Do your best to present yourself to God as one approved, a worker who has no need to be ashamed, rightly handling the word of truth.* 2 TIMOTHY 2:15 (ESV)

When a work truck assigned to a contractor in my department needed repairs, the public works point of contact reached out to question the vehicle's excess mileage. In an internal investigation, the contractor's explanations didn't line up with evidence, and numbers failed to add up correctly. The contractor was put on probation.

Instead of accepting responsibility for his actions, he maligned and spoke inaccuracies about me and other officers. I think what bothered me most was the fact that I thought we were friends. His words and actions hurt deeply. Though my firstborn was just an infant at the time, I vowed to teach Jeremy the value of truthfulness and good moral character according to God's Word.

A trustworthy person exemplifies honesty, reliability, and promise-keeping. A person who can be trusted to do what is right and good. One way to model trustworthiness to your son is to ensure he can trust you in every way. Let him know he can depend on you to keep your word. Sure, things happen beyond our control, but if you promise a trip to the park on Saturday, make sure to follow through. Keep promises made to your spouse and others. Be honest and reliable, always.

Be there for your son when he needs you most, but quite simply—be there! Let your son trust that you'll attend parent meetings at school or baseball games or choir performances. Teaching your son he can trust you enables him to become a trustworthy person of good character.

## Biblical Lessons in Action

- Does your son consider you a trustworthy person? Do you keep your promises? How have you proven your trustworthiness to him? What changes can you make to solidify your reputation as a trustworthy individual?
- Has anyone close to you ever broken your trust by an action or with their words? How can you use that example to teach your son the value of being trustworthy?
- What other examples of trustworthiness can you discuss with your son?
- When your son lets you down in a trust-related issue, plan now to calmly use the incident as a teachable moment, and instead of shaming or embarrassing, ask a question such as, "Can you help me understand why you made that decision?" What other question might you ask to help him learn to value trustworthiness?

## Fairness

*Blessed are those who act justly, who always do what is right.* PSALM 106:3 (NIV)

Whenever we played board games with our little ones, I wanted everyone to be a winner. I stacked the Candy Land deck so each person had a turn at winning, and I divvied up those green houses and red hotels to give everyone the same advantages. Surprisingly, no one ever wanted to play games with me!

When I overheard Jeremy and his cousin playing Monopoly, they playfully argued over properties, recounted fake bills, and questioned spaces moved. They learned a lot about the game of life and had way more fun doing so.

Unlike my games where everybody won and nobody lost, life isn't always fair. The rain falls on the just and the unjust, and bad things happen to good people and vice versa. God never promised an "easy" or "fair" life, but he does expect us to treat others with fairness.

Treating others unfairly is hurtful and insensitive and can escalate to the more serious offense of bullying. Use time spent with your son to point out when others are treated unfairly. Explain to the best of your ability the hurt that injustice causes to encourage your son's empathy. Give him opportunities to practice empathy by serving others in need.

Remind your son of the only one who perfected fairness—Jesus. Point out that God is always fair. His character is never unjust. Help your son strive to be like Jesus and become a young man of good character by teaching him to treat all individuals in a fair way.

## Biblical Lessons in Action

- How can you teach your son to live in an unfair world without becoming bitter or getting discouraged? What helps you remember that God is always good, despite earthly circumstances?
- How do you handle situations you believe are unfair? Are you bold enough to stand up for a situation you deem unjust?
- Think about a recent time you witnessed an injustice. How do you think Jesus would have handled that situation? How can you respond to an unfair situation and show Jesus to those around you?

- Have you ever been treated unfairly? If you had to experience that same situation again, how would your response or words be different this time? What if your son were watching your response, would it still be the same?

# MODEL AND PROMOTE INTEGRITY

**PARENTING PRINCIPLE 10**

MODELING TO YOUR son an uncompromising adherence to ethical values will lay the proper groundwork for his behavioral standards. Integrity means making the right choice for the right reason because it's the right thing to do. Even when it's not the popular decision or the easy one. And most importantly, even when no one else is looking.

Guiding your son to be a person of integrity lays the groundwork for making right choices now and throughout his lifetime. People with integrity hold on to what they value and believe. Therefore, it's critical to make sure your son knows and understands God's Word, believes the Bible, and recognizes Jesus as the Savior from our sins and the essence of our salvation. Modeling and promoting integrity can enhance your son's desire to lead a life of good character that's pleasing to God.

The Bible says in Romans 12:9b–11 (ESV), "Abhor what is evil; hold fast to what is good. Love one another with brotherly affection. Outdo one another in showing honor. Do not be slothful in zeal, be fervent in spirit, serve the Lord."

With this verse as a platform to live by, guide your son to make wise choices, admit wrongdoing, have patience, and be honest as you lead him down the path of integrity. And cheer his successes along the way!

## Make Wise Choices

*If you need wisdom, ask our generous God, and he will give it to you. He will not rebuke you for asking.* JAMES 1:5 (NLT)

Every day, we're faced with choices. Some decisions are less weighty, but many can be life-altering.

When Julie and I completed college, job offers didn't come pouring in like I dreamed. Most employers wanted experience in my field, which I certainly lacked as a new graduate. When I found out about an entomology position in the navy, I made a decision that in hindsight was not thought out nor bathed in prayer. Our sovereign Lord took care of us, thankfully, and it turned out to be the best decision for the two of us and our future family. However, had I sought God's wisdom for making this career decision, I might have saved our marriage a lot of stress and headaches.

Our five-year-old grandson Benaiah doesn't filter all his choices through God just yet, but his parents have done a great job of teaching him to think through his decisions. One weekend during GrandCamp, as my wife calls it, the three of us found a magnolia tree to climb. Having a blast like lemurs stepping from limb to limb, the three of us giggled and climbed. Benaiah started to climb higher and stepped on a thin branch. Before Julie could suggest otherwise, Benaiah said, "I don't think that's a good idea."

Start now teaching your son to let God be his guide for every decision, big or little. The ability to make wise decisions shows integrity. Praise his wise decisions and help him learn from unwise ones. Involve him in your own decision-making, too.

## Biblical Lessons in Action

- When you're faced with a big choice, what steps do you take before making a decision? Do you examine the Bible for an explicit command? Do you listen to the Holy Spirit's guidance? Do you ask God for wisdom?
- How can you involve your spouse and son in your decision-making opportunities? Do you ask trusted mentors or accountability partners to pray for you when making an important decision?
- Think back to a time when you made an unwise choice. How did that affect your family? How did that affect your spiritual life? What could you have done differently?
- In what specific situations have you asked for God's wisdom? How did he provide answers to your dilemma? Have you shared that story with your son?

## Admit Wrongdoing

*One who conceals his wrongdoings will not prosper, but one who confesses and abandons them will find compassion.* PROVERBS 28:13 (NASB)

Once when our boys were little, I stopped their playtime in mud puddles long enough to pose them for a picture with my new camera. When the camera slipped from my hand and landed in the murky mess, a word erupted from my lips that I'm not proud of. I apologized immediately—well, after I retrieved my camera—and we discussed my actions. Years later, Jeb referred to that memory and said, "That one time Mommy said an ugly word."

Not my only wrongdoing, by any stretch of the imagination, but I'm certainly glad that particular transgression is remembered as a single incident.

Children and adults often find it difficult to admit wrongdoing. Fear of punishment or disappointment may be to blame, or perhaps embarrassment or pride. Help your son recognize the need to accept his mistakes and then to make things right. Listen with empathy and understanding, reminding him we all make mistakes. Don't shame or cause more embarrassment, but use the incident as a teachable moment.

Help him understand how the wronged person feels. Teach him to say, "I'm sorry. Can you forgive me?" This may not come naturally at first, and it may not take place immediately following the mistake. Always remember to praise your son when he gets it right!

It helps to recognize that integrity isn't learned all at once. Becoming a person of integrity is a journey that takes time. Be intentional to model the virtues of good character, like admitting wrongdoing.

## Biblical Lessons in Action

- Do you have a hard time admitting when you're wrong? When you hurt someone with your words or actions, are you more prone to ignore and move on or admit wrongdoing and seek forgiveness?
- Are there people in your life that you have a harder time admitting wrongdoing to, like your spouse or son? What can you do to change this attitude? How can you model good character by admitting wrongdoing to family members?
- It's natural to get defensive when we mess up. How can you take ownership of your mistakes and show godly character instead? How can this be a teaching moment for your son?

- Read about the Prodigal Son in Luke 15. How did he confess his sin to his father and to God? How did he try to correct his wrongdoing? Discuss this with your son.

## PRAYER

Dear Jesus, thank you for your mercy and forgiveness. I'm sorry when I do wrong. Please forgive my transgressions that hurt you, my family, or others. Grant me courage to admit when I'm wrong. Give me strong character to acknowledge my sins and grow closer to you each day. Amen.

## Have Patience

*But if we hope for what we do not see, we wait for it with patience.*
ROMANS 8:25 (ESV)

Health care workers, counselors, therapists, and psychologists agree that patience promotes good physical and mental health. Patience also makes people better friends, neighbors, and community members. Patient people achieve goals more often than impatient ones.

Patience tends to be a difficult character behavior to teach but is certainly worthy of giving it your best shot. Give your son opportunities to exercise patience rather than expect instant gratification.

Remember to be patient with your son, spouse, extended family members, and others. Your son observes your behavior and mannerisms. Watch your words, expressions, and actions when your patience is running thin. That car that cut you off on the freeway? Extend patience and pray instead—perhaps the driver of the car is rushing a sick child to the doctor.

Encourage your son to wait patiently on the Lord, too. Remind him answers to prayers may come immediately or may require a great deal of patience.

When I was teaching first grade before becoming a stay-at-home mom, I was so passionate about children's literature, I came home one day and told David, "I want to write a picture book." That was over three decades ago. God led me down different writing paths, but none ever resulted in a children's picture book, no matter how often I prayed.

Until this year, that is.

Soon after this manuscript is due to my publisher, *A Gingerbread House* debuts. It took a lot of patience, but I never gave up on my dream.

# Biblical Lessons in Action

- What circumstances cause you to be impatient? In what areas does your son struggle with patience? How can you give him opportunities to practice patience without frustrating him?
- Who is the most patient person you know? How do they seem healthier, both physically and spiritually? Do you think there's a correlation between their level of patience and their health?
- Think back to a time when you lost your patience in front of your son. Did you use the situation as a teachable moment to remind your son that everyone makes mistakes? What can you do differently the next time a similar circumstance happens?
- Do you have a dream or goal you've patiently prayed about for a long time? What gives you hope about your goal?

## PRAYER

Dear God, grant me patience to navigate whatever comes my way today. When my patience is thin, please strengthen me as only you can. Help me love and serve my family with patience and kindness. Thank you for your patience with me, Lord. Let me model patience with my son. Amen.

# Be Honest

*For we aim at what is honorable not only in the Lord's sight but also in the sight of man.* 2 CORINTHIANS 8:21 (ESV)

Jessica, our youngest, nibbled and picked at her food as a four-year-old. I worried about her health and initiated vitamins for all four kids. At first, Jessica balked, turning up her nose at the gummy vitamins like she did green beans, but she soon complied. Or so I thought.

Call it the fourth child, call it a busy homeschooling season, but this mama totally missed it. One evening after dinner, seven-year-old Jeb whispered, "Mommy, Jessica isn't taking her vitamins. She's lying to you."

I'm not sure what shocked me more—the fact that my four-year-old had learned to lie or the fact that I was too busy to notice her actions.

When I asked about her vitamin, Jessica backed to the garbage can, hands behind her back. She leaned onto the can and said, "I promise I took my vitamin, but please don't look in the trash."

We discussed truthfulness, and she lost privileges before bedtime. Despite faults of his own, Jeb could always be counted on for honesty. He didn't want his sister to get in trouble, but he took it upon himself to worry about her health.

Start early requiring and expecting truth with your son. Be truthful with him always and model honesty around others. Remind your son that honesty is a valued character trait, but more importantly, truth-telling is one of God's commands to his children. Praise your son when he chooses honesty. Show grace when he makes a mistake. Encourage him to right the wrongdoing with truth.

## Biblical Lessons in Action

- Have you ever told a "little" lie that grew and turned into a huge fiasco? How did you rectify that sticky situation?
- Has someone you trusted lied to you in the past? How did the incident affect your relationship with that person? Were you able to salvage the relationship? How does dishonesty affect your ability to trust a person?
- Have you ever thought you could lie to God? Do you have an example you can share with your son? Discuss with your son the powerful point that God knows everything about your life and yet still loves you with an everlasting, unconditional love.
- What Bible stories remind you that "honesty is the best policy"? How can you encourage your son's honesty and celebrate his truthfulness?

## PRAYER

Dear God, forgive my dishonesty. When I'm tempted to bend the truth and tell a lie, let me recognize the Holy Spirit's conviction. Help me strive for honesty in everything I do. Show me how to model honesty for my son and help him strive for honesty as a valued character trait. Amen.

# BUILD HIS RELATIONAL SKILLS

TEACHING YOUR SON how to relate to and care for others prepares him to live in harmony with humanity. Relational skills play a vital role in your son's character development and help him traverse the complexities of the social world. Though the Bible reminds us this world is not our permanent home and Christians should be in the world but not of it, good relational skills will help your son live in harmony with God's creation, both humankind and the environment.

God created us to have relationships. First and foremost, to have a relationship with him through Jesus as our Savior. God wants us to have good relationships with spouses, children, extended family, friends, acquaintances, and strangers, and he gives many directives in the Bible to help us know how to navigate those relationships. Romans 12:18 (ESV) says, "If possible, so far as it depends on you, live peaceably with all." Notice that tiny word "all."

Fostering relational skills in your son, to include social skills, manners, kindness, and compassion, helps him build connections with others, lets others feel valued and loved, and honors God by treating his children the way he's asked in his Word. Mastering these skills is key to maintaining relationships. Encourage your son's faith and character by teaching him to live peaceably with all.

## Social Skills

*Treat people the same way you want them to treat you.* LUKE 6:31 (NASB)

Anxious to find a new church home before we even left California, I reached out to churches in Silverdale, Washington, to determine locations and service times. Once settled, we loaded up four kids and found our way across town. The observant greeter led us to the worship center and said to the usher, "Could you help this family find seats? This is their first time visiting."

The usher responded, "Well, if they want to sit together, they're going to have to get here on time."

Now I'll ask you—which first-time acquaintance showed greater social skills? Obviously that's a rhetorical question. The other part of the story was that I hadn't realized workers had completed the church's parking lot resurfacing since I initially called from

California, and service times had shifted, making us late arrivals when we had thought we were on time.

Healthy social skills help your son become a kind and well-adjusted individual. Start by teaching good communication skills, like maintaining eye contact during conversations, expressing himself effectively, and active listening. Teach him to share, which can be challenging at different developmental stages, but offer many opportunities for practice and praise success often.

Help your son learn that conflict within relationships is inevitable, but resolution with kindness is possible, too. Critical to conflict resolution and healthy relational skills is the ability to empathize—to recognize and understand what others are feeling. Talk often with your son about emotions and how someone else might feel in any given situation. Help your son learn to treat people the way he wants to be treated.

## Biblical Lessons in Action

- How can you model healthy social skills for your son within your home? How might that look different away from home?
- Were your feelings ever stifled, belittled, or shamed as a child? How can you create an environment where your son feels safe to express his feelings and emotions?
- How do you maintain healthy relationships with your spouse, son, friends, coworkers, or occasional acquaintances? How do your social skills in each one of those relationships differ? Which relationship takes the most work on your part?

- How can you use good social skills to show others the love of Jesus? Though the "world" talks often about healthy relationships, how can you prove from the Bible that God was the originator of treating others properly?

## PRAYER

Dear God, strengthen my relationships with those inside my home and beyond. Remind me often how Jesus loved others so well. Help me strive to treat others the way Jesus did. Teach my son to love you first and foremost and to extend that love to humankind. Amen.

## Manners

*And let us not grow weary of doing good, for in due season we will reap, if we do not give up.* GALATIANS 6:9 (ESV)

Growing up in the Deep South, my husband and I learned to say, "Yes ma'am," "No ma'am," "Yes sir," "No sir." So naturally we taught our kids to do the same. Those words from our children were met with acceptance in our communities in North Carolina, Florida, Virginia, and Georgia. We were surprised, however, when we moved to California and women we didn't know personally, on more than one occasion, responded with words like this: "Oh, please don't call me ma'am. I'm not *that* old!" We quickly learned the state of California was rife with well-mannered people, but most of them preferred we left our *ma'am*s back in the South!

Manners may vary from zip codes to countries to cultures, but one thing doesn't change—children and adults with good manners are well-respected and appreciated. Teach your son to display manners and "not grow weary in doing good" to build character. Each time he practices good manners, he strengthens character muscles that will serve him well as he grows into adulthood.

The Bible doesn't use the word "manners," but the Old and New Testaments give instructions about proper etiquette in certain circumstances and directives about the right way to treat people. Teach your son that God values right treatment of others, which means manners are important. Model good manners to help your son follow your examples. Help your son practice courtesy with his words and actions. Correct infractions without shaming and point him toward the right way to respond instead. Reward and celebrate good manners.

## Biblical Lessons in Action

- What manners did your parents enforce? Do you feel like the concept of manners has changed over the years? Do you think that's a good change or a detrimental one?
- Which manners do you enforce more strictly than others with your son? How does your son's use of good manners show respect to family members and people outside the home? Have

you ever spent time around a child or another adult who didn't exhibit good manners? How did that affect your relationship with that person?

- In what way do you think God honors a well-mannered person? How does being well-mannered affect your relationship with God?
- Do an online search of "manners in the Bible" and read some of the passages mentioned, sharing them with your son. Does that change your thoughts about manners?

## PRAYER

Dear God, remind me to use good manners to treat others with love, respect, and kindness. Help me be mindful of my words and actions, especially when I've had a bad day. Let me see others through your lens of love and grant me opportunities to do good to everyone. Amen.

## Kindness

*Each of us should please our neighbors for their good, to build them up.*
ROMANS 15:2 (NIV)

Lightning struck a pine tree near our house during one of last year's hurricanes. The strike jumped from the tree to a nearby transformer, and with a loud BOOM, everyone on the street lost power. Simultaneously, the surge through our house shorted out our security system, an alarm sounded immediately, and a loud robotic voice screamed, "Warning—Fire. Leave the building immediately."

I scrambled to check for smoke or flames while Julie attempted to turn off the alarm's loud screech. Confident it was just a short in the system, we listened to the torrential downpour outside while we hunted lanterns. "Someone's walking up our driveway with a flashlight," my son Jeb said.

"Why in the world is someone out in this weather," I mumbled.

I opened the door to our next-door neighbor. "I heard the fire warning and came to check on you guys," Torry said.

We thanked him profusely.

When the storm subsided, I recalled Torry's actions. Torry and his wife were new to our neighborhood, and we'd barely spoken to them. Wrapped up in our own busy lives, my wife and I hadn't made time for a proper welcome. His kindness that night during a horrific hurricane left quite an impression on our family.

Instill kindness in your son by modeling kindness to those around you. Treat others respectfully and build them up with love. Teach empathy, an understanding of how others feel, to encourage kindness. Kindness is an unforgettable gift you give to others, and it pleases God.

## Biblical Lessons in Action

- Kindness starts in the home and flows outward from there. How does your family exhibit kindness? What does kindness look, sound, and feel like in your family?
- How did Jesus prioritize kindness? Why do you think God values kindness? How are you showing the love of Jesus when you treat others with kindness? What reward do you get from being kind? Discuss this with your son.
- How do you respond when others treat you unkindly? How can responding with kindness to an unkind person reflect Jesus? Who's the kindest person you know?
- What are some acts of kindness you've received over the years that made a lasting impression on you? When have you seen your son extend kindness to others? How did you use that as a teachable moment?

## PRAYER

Heavenly Father, thank you for your never-ending kindness to me. Impress upon me the value of kindness to others. Help me choose kindness always. Let me build up my neighbors and friends, not tear them down. Forgive me when I'm unkind and point me back to Jesus, the kindest of all. Amen.

# Compassion

*Therefore, as God's chosen people, holy and dearly loved, clothe yourselves with compassion, kindness, humility, gentleness and patience.*
COLOSSIANS 3:12 (NIV)

I lost my brother when he was only 47 years old due to complications from addictions he couldn't overcome. I never expected the outpouring of compassion from friends, relatives, and sometimes total strangers. Timothy was such a good man—active in his church, loved serving the Lord, and a kindhearted brother and friend. Alcohol had a strong hold on him, and even though he sought help and had many sober moments, his body couldn't recover from the damage to his liver.

I thought some might blame him, or us—his family who loved him dearly—or even share pithy comments of what he could've done differently.

Yet, I received only compassion. My friends wept for me and with me, and the Lord collected our tears. Lots of them.

Compassion takes empathy one step further. Empathy, the ability to understand and share the feelings of another person, moves to compassion when the empathetic person desires to alleviate another person's pain or improve their well-being in some manner and then acts upon those desires.

Compassion enables us to comfort those around us with care and understanding. Teach your son to radiate compassion to make the world a better place, one compassionate act at a time. Help him understand others' feelings and be mindful of his feelings, too.

Raising your son to be a compassionate child helps him grow into an engaged, caring young man. Reminding him that God's Word tells us to clothe ourselves in compassion strengthens his relationship with the Lord and builds character muscles, too.

## Biblical Lessons in Action

- Think about a recent time someone showed you genuine compassion. Did that act change your situation? How did that person's kindness affect your relationship with God? With that person?
- When do you find it easy to offer compassion? Are there times when you find it hard to be compassionate? Is it difficult for you to show compassion to someone who's hurt you in the past? Or maybe to someone you struggle to like? Use these questions as a springboard to discuss compassion with your son.
- Think about a recent time you offered compassion. What motivated you to act that way? Does showing compassion strengthen your relationship with God?
- What practical steps can you take at home to teach your son empathy? What opportunities can you offer your son to learn about and show compassion?

## PRAYER

Dear God, thank you for the mercy and compassion you show me in my times of need. Thank you for Jesus' compassion on the cross to die a death he didn't deserve to save me from the sins of the world. Fill my heart with compassion to offer comfort to those around me. Amen.

# WELCOME PARENTING PARTNERSHIPS

ASSISTANCE FROM OTHERS who present godly examples to your son supports your son's spiritual journey and reinforces family values. As parents, we often want to feel like we can "do it all." We want to be Super Dad or Wonder Mom. We might feel inadequate if we consider asking for help. Accepting help from others doesn't reveal inadequacies. In fact, the opposite is true. Welcoming parenting partnerships displays wisdom in knowing when to seek support.

God desires his children to lend a hand and take care of one another. Galatians 6:2 (ESV) says, "Bear one another's burdens, and so fulfill the law of Christ." Easing the burden of another in obedience to God draws us closer to him. Asking for and accepting assistance from others who have a strong relationship with the Lord creates an environment where others who love your son can present godly examples of Christian life, support your son's spiritual journey, and reinforce family values.

Choose carefully the circle of family and friends who'll spend time with your son and pour into his faith walk. Seek godly people who'll love your son well. Be intentional with parenting partnerships by showing a united front with your parenting partner, accepting assistance from extended family members, valuing the support of friends and church members, and recognizing God as the ultimate parenting partner.

## Show a United Front with Your Parenting Partner

*Let no corrupting talk come out of your mouths, but only such as is good for building up, as fits the occasion, that it may give grace to those who hear.* EPHESIANS 4:29 (ESV)

Sometimes parenting partners reside in different homes. But hopefully with a deep love for your son and an abiding love for Christ, you can work together with your son's best interest in mind. If you are married to your son's other parent or have a good co-parenting relationship with them, your united parenting front is a gift that builds a solid foundation for your son's growth and development. Build up your co-parent partner, in word and deed, just as God desires.

If you are parenting your son on your own, build up the other parent, caregiver, or parenting support members in your community of family and friends who desire to see your son grow and develop into a godly young man of good character. Speak highly of them, make every attempt not to argue with that person in front of your son, and encourage them often.

Plan to make decisions together with your parenting partner or other supportive caregiver. When you make decisions together or establish rules that affect your son, stay consistent. Inconsistencies confuse your son and challenge relationships. Parenting should never be a "good parent, bad parent" situation.

Obviously, you'll differ in opinions with your parenting partner at times. Make every effort to solve those differences in private, but it's okay to let your son know you and your partner don't always see eye to eye. Perfect relationships aren't normal, and teaching your son how to handle conflict is part of growing up.

Let your son see and hear you praying through decisions, too. Prove to him with your words and actions that you and your parenting partner are a team, his biggest cheerleaders, and greatest advocates! Make sure he knows how happy you are that God chose the two of you to be his parents.

## Biblical Lessons in Action

- How does parenting as a united front benefit your relationship with your son's other parent or supportive member of your son's community of caregivers? How does that relationship benefit your son? What parenting issue causes the most angst between you and your co-parent?

- Do you and your son's prominent support system members involve God in your decision-making? What role does his Word, the Bible, play in the decisions and choices you make? Do you pray with your son's other primary parenting person daily?
- How can you strengthen your parenting team? How do you let others on your parenting team know you value and appreciate them?
- Have you thanked your parenting team recently? How do you support and encourage your spouse or parenting team?

## PRAYER

Dear God, thank you for my parenting team who helps me love my son well. Let no corrupting talk come out of my mouth. Give me only words of love and support that will build up those who desire to raise my son to be a godly man. Help us parent well and love you even more. Amen.

## Accept Assistance from Extended Family

*Anyone who does not provide for their relatives, and especially for their own household, has denied the faith and is worse than an unbeliever.*
1 TIMOTHY 5:8 (NIV)

Extended family members graciously served our family over the years. Though my husband's military career kept us hopping from state to state, our parents and siblings invariably showed up to help us on many occasions.

My sister came to stay for a week when my doctor's orders put me on bed rest. We still laugh about the afternoon she drove me to an appointment, and when we returned, I realized I'd locked us out of the house. Fortunately, the bathroom window was open slightly. Unfortunately, eight-months-pregnant me obviously couldn't climb! LeeAnn hoisted herself in, tried to balance on the toilet with one foot, swung the other leg over . . . and her foot promptly slipped into the toilet.

When Jeremy's x-rays revealed pneumonia, my mom and dad stepped in to take care of toddler Jenifer while Jeremy was hospitalized. And when baby number four arrived in California, my mother-in-law's presence kept the house running smoothly for our two sons and other daughter.

Our extended family members have loved our children well, supported us during challenging circumstances, provided for us physically and emotionally, and exemplified strong faith in Jesus Christ. Their spiritual witness to our children undergirded our beliefs and solidified our kids' faith.

Allow assistance from your extended family members to support your son's spiritual journey and reinforce family values. If extended family relationships are not the strong ties you desire or if family members live too far away to provide assistance, consider seeking that kind of relationship with godly church members or neighbors.

## Biblical Lessons in Action

- What roles have extended family members played in raising your son? Do you wish those relationships could be different? Do your extended family members have a relationship with Christ? Have you shared the gospel with those who don't?
- When life gets overwhelming, who do you call on most often for assistance with your son? How do those relationships strengthen your son's faith walk?
- Who in your family is the most helpful to your parenting journey? What qualities does that person exhibit that you hope your son will emulate?
- Have you recently offered assistance to extended family members? Your parents, siblings, or in-laws? How does taking care of extended family members show obedience to God and soften your son's heart for others?

## PRAYER

Dear God, thank you for the family you gave me, extended family and immediate family. Teach me ways to show my appreciation and gratitude to family members. Let my life reflect Jesus to those I hold most dear. Help me provide for my relatives in whatever way you lead me. Amen.

## Value Support of Friends and Church

*So encourage each other and build each other up, just as you are already doing.* 1 THESSALONIANS 5:11 (NLT)

Being completely immersed in a local church body of fellowship when our children were growing up solidified their faith and strengthened their spiritual journey exponentially. And it also gave Jeb a ride home from church when he was forgotten!

The third of four children, Jeb considers himself "the middle child." He decided on that moniker when my husband and I accidentally left him at church. You see, it happened like this . . .

We often hosted youth events for our kiddos and their friends following the Sunday evening service. I hurried home after the service to prepare the baked potato bar kids looked forward to. I mistakenly thought Jeb was catching a ride home with Jeremy, who'd driven his siblings to church for choir practice prior to the service. And Jeremy assumed Jeb was with me.

Fortunately, our best friends left the service after me. My friend Paula called while I was en route. "Just checking to see if you'd like me to bring Jeb home when I come to your house for dinner." I laughed . . . because it wasn't the first time our best friends had to rescue "the middle child."

Those dear friends, other close church friends, and beloved pastors and their wives played significant, monumental roles in helping us raise our children. Sunday school volunteers mentored the kids and backed up our teachings. Pastors extolled godly wisdom and biblical truths. Friends provided godly fellowship and fun.

Assistance, encouragement, and love from precious friends and church members has blessed our family immeasurably.

## Biblical Lessons in Action

- How have friends and fellow church members helped you in your parenting journey? In what ways have those individuals strengthened your walk with the Lord? How have they influenced your son's faith journey?
- What is your favorite part about being involved in a fellowship of other believers? How does surrounding yourself with God's people make your parenting journey lighter and more enjoyable?
- What friend could you call on at any given moment, night or day, that would be there for you in a heartbeat? Point out to your son the qualities in that person that make them a good friend. How can you pay that relationship forward and be a good friend to others?
- What friends have helped "bear your burdens" in the past? Do you bear others' burdens?

## Recognize God as the Ultimate Parenting Partner

*So do not fear, for I am with you; do not be dismayed, for I am your God. I will strengthen you and help you; I will uphold you with my righteous right hand.* ISAIAH 41:10 (NIV)

"I'll be deploying to the Gulf in just a couple of weeks," David announced, just prior to what we now call Operation Desert Storm and the Gulf War. "I leave before Christmas." Jeremy was only eighteen months old at the time. I was devastated. And terrified.

I felt so alone when David left, even though a toddler shadowed me everywhere. God had been my Heavenly Father for as long as I could remember; I asked Jesus to be my Savior when I was nine years old. But until that time, I'm not sure I fully comprehended how much I needed the Lord in my life. Those six months were the closest I'd ever come to being a single parent. I knew several single moms prior to his deployment, and I always thought they had the hardest job in the world!

I clung to God like never before. I needed his strength every day, every minute. I hung on to verses that reminded me God was with me and would never leave me. On days I felt crippled with fear for my husband's safety, I imagined God physically holding me upright with his righteous right hand.

During David's deployment, I realized God is my ultimate parenting partner. He loves my children far more than I ever could. He's just a prayer away to help me make decisions and to guide me. He wants good for me and my children. He'll never leave me nor my children. His love is everlasting and unconditional. I'm grateful and love him so much.

## Biblical Lessons in Action

- What role do you feel like God displays most in your family: Heavenly Father, co-parent, or head of the household? Does he take on a different role according to the circumstances?
- Can you feel the Holy Spirit's nudges as you make parental decisions? If not, what can help you sense those nudges more readily?
- How does your relationship with God point your son to an intimate relationship with God? What situations open discussions with your son about obedience to God and listening to him?
- Are God and his instructions your model as a parent? How's that going for you? Do you remember to use the Bible like a blueprint for raising your son?

## PRAYER

Lord, you are the perfect parent. Let me turn to you as my ultimate parenting partner to guide me on this journey. You are my strength, God. I cannot parent without you. As much as I love my son, I know you love him immeasurably more. Thank you, God, for your love. Amen.

# PARENTING PRINCIPLE 13 | TREASURE FORGIVENESS

CHRIST MADE THE ultimate sacrifice for forgiveness of sins if you confess and turn away from them. Romans 3:23–24 (NLT) says, "For everyone has sinned; we all fall short of God's glorious standard. Yet God, in his grace, freely makes us right in his sight. He did this through Christ Jesus when he freed us from the penalty for our sins."

Although Jesus never sinned, he took on the sins of the world—past, present, and future—and paid the ultimate sacrifice by his death on the cross. Believing in Jesus as God's Son, accepting him as our Savior, gives us eternal life in heaven. Our job is to confess our sins and repent, which means to turn away from those sins.

Because Christ bridged this gap for us to allow forgiveness of our sins, God demands that we forgive others. When we focus on what God did for us through Christ's sacrifice to secure our forgiveness, the burden of forgiving others lessens.

Forgiveness requires faith—we need God's strength to help us. We're not capable of forgiving on our own. Forgiving someone who wronged us is just hard! Help your son treasure forgiveness by first explaining "original sin." Then discuss Christ's sacrifice and forgiveness and emphasize the importance of forgiving others. And you'll need to forgive your son over and over.

## Explain "Original Sin" to Your Son

*Yes, Adam's one sin brings condemnation for everyone, but Christ's one act of righteousness brings a right relationship with God and new life for everyone.* ROMANS 5:18 (NLT)

A difficult concept for some children to understand, and many adults for that matter, is the idea of original sin. It's important to help your son understand his need for forgiveness in relation to Adam's sin shortly after the creation of the world.

When God first created humankind, he did so in a perfect world. The world he'd just created in all its magnificence. With Adam and Eve's disobedience to God in Eden, sin entered the world and with it came death and destruction. Because we are all descendants of Adam, human beings inherit Adam's original sin.

Humankind is born sinful and in need of a Savior. Teach your son that even though he bears the image of God, he is sinful from birth due to original sin. In addition to original sin, your son and every inhabitant on the planet is sinful by nature and guilty of actual sins.

Our Heavenly Father is perfect, holy, and good. We cannot come into the presence of God's holiness as tarnished sinners. Jesus' gift to us on the cross covered our sins and brought us into a right relationship with God. We are forgiven of our sins—the inherited ones through original sin and the willful disobedience of our actual sins—because of Jesus.

Teach your son to treasure and value the gift of forgiveness displayed to us on the cross by the only person who ever lived a sinless life. Remind him that with Christ we have a new life, forgiven and clean.

## Biblical Lessons in Action

- Do you struggle with the idea of "original sin" as it relates to you and your need for a Savior?
- How old were you when you truly comprehended what it meant to be a sinner? In what ways did you feel "washed clean" when you accepted Jesus as your personal Savior? Have you shared these details with your son?
- How easy is it for you to ask your son for forgiveness, like when you've lost your temper, broken a promise, or been unfair? Is there something you should address with your son today?
- If you could talk to Adam and Eve about their historical moment in the Garden of Eden, what do you think you'd say? Do you question their decision back then while living in a perfect world?

## Christ's Sacrifice and Forgiveness

*If we confess our sins, he is faithful and just to forgive us our sins and to cleanse us from all unrighteousness.* 1 JOHN 1:9 (ESV)

For a middle school youth event, Jeremy dressed up like his favorite Sunday school teacher for costume night. The teacher was impressed and laughed, but the teacher's son, also in the youth group, was offended. Later that night, I received a phone call from the Sunday school teacher's wife, an acquaintance who lived not far from us in Silverdale. She scolded and berated me for Jeremy's actions. I apologized and tried my best to assure her that Jeremy chose to dress up like her husband because of his admiration for his favorite teacher.

Jeremy apologized to the teacher and his son later and quickly forgave the teacher's wife. I struggled with her hurtful words.

Several weeks later, our pastor preached about forgiveness. Afterward, I felt a tap on my back. I turned to see the teacher's wife, and with tears in her eyes, she said, "Please forgive me." She explained briefly that the incident angered her because of a hurtful situation in her past. She gave me a big hug, a hug that felt like the warmth of Jesus.

Jesus, sinless and perfect, made the ultimate sacrifice for the forgiveness of humankind's sins. When we confess our sins, God sees our sins no more. We are made clean because of the blood of Jesus. His righteousness, not ours, makes us right before God.

Teach your son to confess his sins to God. Help him also learn to seek forgiveness of those he's wronged. Remind him of that warm-hug feeling of forgiveness!

## Biblical Lessons in Action

- Take time to read and think about Jesus' sacrifice as told in one of the Gospels. You might try Matthew 27, Mark 15, Luke 23, or John 19. Have you considered what it means to "take up your cross and follow Jesus"?
- Do you feel worthy of the sacrifice Jesus made for you? Is there something in your personal life you should "sacrifice" that would help you grow in your faith?
- How can you share the crucifixion story with your son, in an age-appropriate way, to help him recognize Jesus' sacrifice and trust God's magnificent love simultaneously?
- What practical steps can you take to help your son learn to confess his shortcomings to God and receive his forgiveness? Ask your son to describe what it feels like to be forgiven.

## The Importance of Forgiving Others

*For if you forgive others their trespasses, your heavenly Father will also forgive you.* MATTHEW 6:14 (ESV)

Willingly choosing to forgive someone who hurts us is hard. However, with God's strength, we can forgive those who cause us pain. Because Jesus' death on the cross made the way for us to be forgiven, it's the least we can do in return for his sacrifice. And because we love God, we should want to obey his instructions to forgive others.

We don't have to condone a person's actions to forgive them. And in certain circumstances, that person who wrongs us may have to earn our trust again. But when we forgive others, we experience peace and let go of bitterness. We can turn the issue over to God, but our forgiveness makes us emotionally healthier and paves the way for mended relationships. Forgiveness is an outward sign of faith in God and strong moral character. It's always the right thing to do and what we're instructed to do.

Some of Jeb's new baseball teammates poked fun at his stature—he was one of the shorter ones on his team when he was just seven years old—and made jokes about his left-handedness. To some, it may have come across as "boys will be boys" teasing, but it bordered on bullying in my opinion.

This mommy wanted to tattle and demand a team change, but Jeb halted me. "I forgive them, Mommy. I'm short, but I'm gonna grow." With just a few practices, Jeb showed his teammates his speed, agility, and bunting abilities. Teasing turned to admiration, and Jeb formed friendships that lasted for years.

## Biblical Lessons in Action

- Is there someone with whom you've harbored unforgiveness of a wrong from the past? What do you think is keeping you from forgiving that person? What steps can you take to move toward healing and freedom that comes from forgiveness?
- How can you use forgiveness and unforgiveness from the past to teach your son valuable lessons about forgiving others? About seeking forgiveness for wrong actions?
- Pick a favorite Old Testament story to read with your son. Talk about the forgiveness element of the story.
- Is there a sin you need to confess and seek forgiveness for? When you genuinely seek forgiveness, do you feel forgiven? Do you believe that your sins are wiped clean?

## Forgive Your Son, Over and Over

*Even if they sin against you seven times in a day and seven times come back to you saying "I repent," you must forgive them.* LUKE 17:4 (NIV)

Jeremy loved building and creating with Legos. With dexterity and unending creativity, he fashioned intricate pieces of three-dimensional art, projects that took hours to put together. And yet, kindhearted Jeremy responded affirmatively each time Jeb, six years younger, asked to play with his creation.

Without fail, Jeb's five-year-old fingers accidentally dismantled Jeremy's creations each time. Though Jeremy would often get angry initially, he forgave quickly . . . and said yes the next time Jeb asked to play with his creative piece.

As the granddaddy who is often asked to build and create various masterpieces for his five-year-old grandson, I'm recognizing even more how kind Jeremy was to forgive destroyed creations over and over.

God doesn't put a limit on the number of times we should forgive someone. Over and over and over—seven times over and then some. Your son—and others—may test your patience with repeated infractions. Your job as a parent is to continue to model forgiveness, over and over, so that your son can learn to forgive others repeatedly.

God is our example of forgiving others in every way. From forgiving quickly, to forgiving repeatedly, to forgiving completely with no record of wrongs. Help your son practice forgiving others. Remind him that the person whom he's forgiving may not ask for forgiveness. Teach him to forgive anyway.

When your son messes up, help him learn to say, "I'm sorry. Will you please forgive me?" Being willing to forgive your son over and over models God's grace and forgiveness.

## Biblical Lessons in Action

- Why is forgiveness hard? Is it harder for you to forgive an acquaintance or a close family member? Why do you think that's so?
- Is there a particular fault your son struggles with that needs repeated forgiveness? How does modeling that forgiveness help your son understand God's forgiveness?
- Have you ever held on to bitterness or held a grudge against someone who wronged you, even though you claimed you forgave that person? How did your lack of forgiveness affect your relationship with that person? Your relationship with God?

- Did you get into trouble for repeated mistakes as a child? Did your parents forgive each time? How do you assure your son of your unconditional, unending love, especially when he's in trouble for repeated disobedience?

## PRAYER

God, help me remember how often you forgive me when I get impatient with my son's repeated offenses. Help me forgive over and over. That's what you do, Lord, and I'm so grateful. Help me teach my son to forgive often. Thank you for forgiveness and the promise of eternity in heaven with you. Amen.

# PARENTING PRINCIPLE 14 | SPEND TIME WITH YOUR SON

INVESTING YOURSELF IN your son's life will show him how much you love and care for him. Alarming statistics suggest most families spend just slightly over half an hour of intentional time together daily. Equally staggering statistics point out that children spend three times that many minutes, or more, on devices or some sort of media per day. Family dynamics, job situations, and the advances of technology contribute greatly to these statistics, but don't negate the need or desire your son has for undivided attention from his parents.

We humans tend to make time for things we value and treasure. Psalm 127:3 (NLT) says, "Children are a gift from the LORD; they are a reward from him." Are you treating your son like he is a treasured and valued gift from God? Spending time with your son by investing in his life will assure him of your love and care. Evidence of your love teaches him about God's love and strengthens his relationship with Jesus. The confidence your son receives from a secure relationship with his parents builds character and boosts self-esteem.

Invest in your son deliberately with your time by communicating intentionally with him, getting involved in his activities, supporting and joining him in his interests and hobbies, and knowing and approving of those who influence him.

## Intentional Communication

*My dear brothers and sisters, take note of this: Everyone should be quick to listen, slow to speak and slow to become angry.* JAMES 1:19 (NIV)

By the time Jeremy was three years old, he could name practically every dinosaur imaginable. His earliest fascinations included sea creatures and dinosaurs. David's science background fueled Jeremy's passions, but as the playmate while Daddy worked, I had to learn the lingo to communicate with my little guy.

My husband and I agree, Jeremy's creativity came from me. So, most mornings found the two of us playing with some sort of animal toy in an adventurous setting. Jeremy's vivid imagination created the dialogue for both of us. Jeremy would let one of his creatures talk in a lengthy paragraph, and then he'd announce, "Okay, Mommy, now you say . . ." and he'd feed the words to me. Our communication then may have been one-sided, but it sure set a pattern for deep conversations in the coming years.

Talk with your son often and start early! Ask lots of questions and be quick to listen intently to the answers. Make eye contact, and as often as possible, get down on your son's level to make eye contact more meaningful. Pay attention to verbal and nonverbal communication between you and your son. Learn to read cues that might express his emotions more than his actual words. Talk about things your son enjoys and share your passions, too.

Let your son know you enjoy conversations with him and especially love hearing about his day at school or day care or extracurricular activities. Value and listen to his opinions and ideas. Show him you are genuinely interested in his words!

## Biblical Lessons in Action

- How can you open the lines of communication with your son? Is there anything that hampers productive conversation with your son?

- Is there a consistent time and place you can talk to your son without distractions or interruptions? Do you consider incentives to open up conversation, like a snack or cup of hot chocolate?

- Have you discussed your son's dreams or goals recently? If the answer is yes, have you researched the dreams or goals to see how you might provide input for dialogue or even how you might enable him to realize a short-term goal?

- What can you say to your son to build him up or help him feel loved and appreciated? What has he done recently that you can brag about?

## PRAYER

Dear God, show me how to communicate with my son more effectively and intentionally to remind him of my love. Help me model communication with you to my son to strengthen my relationship with you, to help me be a better parent, and to grow his faith and trust in you, too. Amen.

## Involved and Present

*Children's children are a crown to the aged, and parents are the pride of their children.* PROVERBS 17:6 (NIV)

As much as time allows, get involved in your son's activities, and stay involved. Kids whose parents are actively involved in their school events or other activities tend to do better in those activities and exhibit more confidence. Parental involvement in school, sports activities, or other extracurricular events encourages a child to try harder or excel, knowing the parent is actively engaged and watching.

Being involved in your son's life—at church, school, and other places—gives you the chance to know his friends and the influential adults he spends time around. It also opens up the lines of communication, because you can actively talk about those activities you're familiar with.

Though we're not advocating helicopter parenting, active involvement with your son's activities offers opportunities to bond, grow closer, and have fun together. Spending time with your son in various activities stimulates healthy spiritual conversations as you discuss with your son how these events relate to Jesus and God's Word.

And, bottom line—most kids take great pride in their parents' presence at events outside the home. On a few occasions, our preteen and teenage sons verbally scoffed at the "uncoolness" of our participation, but they soon recognized the benefits and were openly glad to have us around.

Some of the ways to get involved in your son's activities could include providing snacks for sports teams, helping backstage during a theater production, teaching Sunday school classes, joining him at school during lunchtime, giving a presentation in his classroom, chaperoning church activities or mission trips, and more.

## Biblical Lessons in Action

- Have you checked into volunteer opportunities at your son's school or homeschool co-op? Are there any positions that meet your schedule and skills? What's holding you back?

- What volunteer positions at church do you actively take part in that enable you to spend more time with your son? What gifts, talents, or expertise do you possess that your son's teacher would enjoy sharing with the classroom?
- Did your parents take an active role in your life when you were a child? How did it make you feel to have their support (or their lack of support)? How can you improve on those dynamics with your son's activities to build a healthy relationship?
- In what ways do you want your son to be proud of you?

## PRAYER

Dearest Heavenly Father, thank you for the gift of my son. Help me be intentional to spend quality time with him each day. Show me ways to get involved in his activities that will strengthen our parent-son relationship and will give me opportunities to point him to you. Amen.

## Interests and Hobbies

*Behold, how good and pleasant it is when brothers dwell in unity.*
PSALM 133:1 (ESV)

Jeb and I looked forward every year to the father-son freeze-out during his years of scouting adventures. Held in January at a camp a few hours away, we were often cold as we huddled in our two-man tent, but South Georgia winters are not as brutal as other places could've been.

During the freeze-out, father-and-son teams competed in various mental and physical challenges. Jeb and I worked well together—I used my work-related science prowess, and he tapped into his memorization abilities and homeschool wisdom. We aced "name the books of the Bible in order," "name all the state capitals," "tree identification by bark," "bird identification by feathers," and more.

Psalm 133:1 above speaks of "brothers" dwelling in unity in a slightly different meaning, but I believe God intends for fathers and sons (and mothers and sons) to dwell in unity. Supporting my son's scouting interests fit that bill perfectly for us, and we genuinely had fun, too. Even if we did sleep cold each night! During those short weekends, Jeb and I united as a team, which helped us bond in ways that spilled over into other aspects of our life and relationship.

As parents, we can encourage our sons' interests and hobbies to teach lifelong skills, encourage social, emotional, and academic growth, improve self-esteem, and help them relate those activities to their own spiritual growth and development. Getting involved in your son's interests is another way of showing your son how much you love him.

## Biblical Lessons in Action

- What are your son's interests and hobbies? Do you take an active role in those activities with him? How do those relate to your interests and hobbies?
- What is your favorite thing to do with your son? How can that activity strengthen your son's relationship with God? How can you use that time together to open the door for spiritual conversations?
- In your opinion, what does it mean to "dwell in unity" with a fellow believer? What does it look like when your family dwells in unity?
- How can your son's interests and hobbies play a vital role in his relationship with Jesus? How can those activities build good character? What other ways can you encourage your son's interests and hobbies besides volunteering with those activities?

## PRAYER

Dear God, thank you for my passions and hobbies that make life fun and interesting. Help me keep those in perspective, God, making your kingdom work my top priority. Show me how to take an active role in my son's interests and hobbies that will ultimately point him to you in every way. Amen.

# Knowing and Approving Influences

*Do not be deceived: "Bad company corrupts good character."*
1 CORINTHIANS 15:33 (BSB)

When Jeremy caused angst in our household due to a bit of teen-age drama, David and I offered sound advice for a solution. Well, we considered our words to be sound, wise, biblical suggestions. Jeremy answered respectfully, but he might as well have said, "You don't get it because you're old. You can't relate to my high school issues."

A week or so later, Jeremy began the conversation with, "I talked with Mr. Ray about the situation with my friends." Ray, Jeremy's Sunday school teacher whom he greatly admired, was a dear friend of ours. Jeremy proceeded to tell us, almost word for word, the "sound and wise" biblical advice we'd offered the previous week. Suddenly, those words were the perfect solution to Jeremy's problem.

David and I listened intently and didn't bother to point out we'd shared the same advice. But later that night, David and I thanked God for friends and teachers like Ray who pour into the lives of our children, influence them for God's kingdom, and support our Christian parenting.

As your son grows into a young man, he'll have lots of people who'll influence his thoughts, decisions, and actions. Make every effort to know personally the people who are influencing your son. Get to know schoolteachers, church leaders, church volunteers, older and same-age friends, parents of friends, and so on. As much as you can control, make sure those folks are pouring the love of Christ into your son and building good character, not corrupting it.

## Biblical Lessons in Action

- Jot down the people in your son's life who have the potential to influence him. Do you know each one personally? What kind of relationship do you have with each one? Do you know anything about their walk with the Lord?
- Who were the biggest influences on you as a child and teenager? Were those people good influences? Or would you say they corrupted your character? What can you learn from each of those situations that will help you with those who influence your son?
- How much time do you spend each week investing in your son's life by communicating with him? By getting involved with his activities? By supporting his interests and hobbies? By getting to know who and what influences him?
- How does God influence your thoughts, words, and actions?

## PRAYER

Dear God, protect my family from negative influences. Surround my family with adults and peers who teach us more about Jesus, strengthen our faith, and solidify good character. Thank you for the mentors and influences in our lives who love our family and love you even more! Amen.

# PARENTING PRINCIPLE 15

# LOVE YOUR SON LIKE JESUS DOES

SHOWING YOUR SON that you love him unconditionally reflects the unshakable love of God. Jesus taught us about God's unconditional, unshakable love and provides the greatest example of love humankind has ever known. Jesus loved with his whole heart: tirelessly, sacrificially, selflessly, and intentionally. With kindness, compassion, and patience and with a desire for our good and God's glory. Jesus loves *your* son like that!

Love your son with the gusto and depth of Jesus. Let everything you do with your son point him to God. Jesus showed us the ultimate design for loving our sons by the way he loved. John 13:34 (NIV) says, "A new command I give you: Love one another. As I have loved you, so you must love one another." Jesus said love others—including your son—the way he loved others.

Will we make mistakes? Sure! No one but Jesus has ever lived a perfect life. But we can strive every day to love more like Jesus. Love your son unconditionally and show God's unshakable love by providing for your son, not provoking him, affirming him often, and loving him well. Remember the truth of who Jesus is and what he did for you and be a living example of Jesus for your son.

## Provide

*After all, children don't provide for their parents. Rather, parents provide for their children.* 2 CORINTHIANS 12:14B (NLT)

Paul responds to church members in Corinth with the words above in reference to the Corinthians' desire to give money to Paul for financial support of his ministry. Paul did not want to be a financial burden on the people of Corinth. We typically think of this verse advocating the financial support of children by their parents. But because Paul saw himself as the spiritual father of the believers in Corinth and provided for their spiritual needs first and foremost, I think we can infer Paul meant more than just meeting financial needs.

As Christian parents, our primary provision for our sons should be leading them to Jesus. Raising your son to know and love Jesus and accept him as his personal Savior is vitally important. Life-and-death important, as a matter of fact.

Other key areas of provision include physical needs like food, shelter, clothing, medical care, and safety, as well as educational and emotional needs. Of course, it goes without saying that parents and guardians should provide love for their son. Aim to love your son like Jesus loves your son, unconditionally and unabashedly with a fierce, never-ending depth.

Rather than material goods, concentrate on encouraging his relationship with Jesus Christ, the greatest inheritance he could ever receive. Create an environment of a loving home where your son feels safe, physically and emotionally. As instructed by God's Word, provide for his needs to enable him to grow into a godly young man of strong faith and character.

## Biblical Lessons in Action

- How does God meet every one of your needs? When recently has God gone above meeting your needs and given you the extra treat of a "want" or "fulfilled dream"?
- Make a list of God's provisions over the last month or so. Have you remembered to thank him for the items on your list? How can you be more grateful for the ways God provides for your family?
- How can you be a good steward of the things God has given you? How can you remind your son that every good gift comes from God?
- In what ways does God help you provide for your son? Is there an unmet need that you struggle to take care of? What steps can you take to change that?

## Don't Provoke

*Fathers, do not antagonize your children, so that they will not become discouraged.* COLOSSIANS 3:21 (NASB)

Tall for his age, Benaiah often gravitated toward kids slightly older than him. Which often meant our sweet four-year-old grandson couldn't do some of the same playground activities as the other boys his same height. When he couldn't master the rungs of the monkey bars or jump from one soft mushroom pad to the next or put the pegs in the right spot on the large wooden puzzle, Benaiah despaired and gave up. His sadness was palpable. Discouraged, he usually pulled away from the other kids and sat alone, just watching the activity.

Most of the time, I could coerce him into persevering. I said often, "It's okay. Sometimes that happens, and we have to just keep trying." Many times, with just one more try, he accomplished his goal, even if the older kids had moved on to something else.

Discouraged children often give up, quit trying, retreat into themselves, or even rebel, act out, and seek negative means for attention. It was hard watching my grandson's discouragement, and I never want to be the catalyst for tearing him down emotionally, physically, mentally, or spiritually by provoking him.

Various translations of Colossians 3:21 warn fathers (and, we can assume, mothers, grandparents, and other adult guardians and mentors) not to embitter, aggravate, provoke, antagonize, or exasperate children. Others that might fit could include embarrass, belittle, ignore, neglect, shame, or nag. Whichever verb resonates with you most, use it as a reminder to love your son like Jesus and not provoke him, lest he become discouraged.

## Biblical Lessons in Action

- What steps can you take to ensure you don't exasperate your son? What are some instances in the past where your words or actions provoked your son? How can you respond differently to a similar situation in the future?
- What signs or hints does your son give you, physically or verbally, when he is nearing exasperation? How can you use those clues to defuse the situation?
- Taking your son's age into consideration, what conversations can you have about ways to avoid provoking him? How will you point out that every parent makes mistakes sometimes? How can you assure him that you'll keep his feelings and emotions in mind when parenting him?

## Reassuring Affirmations

*I praise You, for I am fearfully and wonderfully made. Marvelous are Your works, and I know this very well.* PSALM 139:14 (BSB)

How often do you affirm your son? An affirmation can be defined as words or actions that show encouragement, recognition, approval, or support. Your son is fearfully and wonderfully made by the Creator God, the Almighty Father, the Savior of the world. Isn't your son worth affirming regularly?

When our kids were growing up, I liked celebrating these silly holidays that someone somewhere came up with. And my favorite part of the celebration often included a note of affirmation. For National Cheese Day, I wrote this note to my son: "I think you're grate!" I'd place the note on the kitchen table next to my grater, and we'd celebrate the day with a string cheese snack.

I initiated the holiday celebrations before Jeb was old enough to read my affirmations, but he still got it! I remember when I wrote this note and placed it next to a pack of gum for National Chewing Gum Day: "Let's stick together forever!" The first one to wake up, Jeb snatched the pack of gum and skipped to his brother's room, singing, "It's Happy Gum Day!"

Positive affirmations benefit your son in a number of ways. Your genuine and specific words give him confidence and a healthy self-esteem to grow into a mature young man. Affirmations allow him to persevere and feel proud of his accomplishments. Affirming words instill positivity and encourage hope.

But bottom line, affirmations show your love and devotion and help him truly know he is fearfully and wonderfully made by God.

## Biblical Lessons in Action

- Were you raised by parents who affirmed you often? How did those affirmations strengthen your faith and build your character? Conversely, how did the lack of affirmations affect your youth and adulthood?
- What effects have you seen in your son when you give him affirmations? What type of affirmations work best with him? After modeling affirmation to your son, have you noticed him returning the encouragement and support? How does that make you feel?
- What are your favorite Bible verses that feel like personal affirmations from God? Have you shared those affirmations of love and encouragement with your son?

- Consider making an extensive list of positive affirmations to keep in mind for frequent usage. How can you be intentional to affirm your son often?

## Love Him Well

*Let all that you do be done in love.* 1 CORINTHIANS 16:14 (ESV)

What a privilege and honor to be chosen by God to raise and nurture a precious little boy, from infant to toddler, from preschooler to adolescent, and from teenager to young adult. God chose you specifically to raise your son. When you love your son well, your ultimate goal is to ensure his faith and relationship with Jesus. Raising your son to love Jesus and grow into a young man of strong character is the greatest gift you could offer him.

Love your son well every day. There will be some days that "life" gets in the way, and you may think you didn't hit the mark. Many days will be hard and challenging. But find those moments. No matter how difficult the day, make sure to find those moments to intentionally love your son with great gusto and passion.

Make time to talk daily. Kids are more likely to make wise choices when they stay connected to you and to other family members. Say "I love you" often and show love regularly, too.

Play, have fun, go on adventures, spend time together, discipline in love, affirm, share, pray, create, respect, and grow together.

Make sure your son knows you value and adore him. Let him know you enjoy spending time with him. Treat him like the treasure from God that he is. Love your son like Jesus does, with an unconditional love that reflects the unshakable love of God.

Enjoy a wonderful relationship with your son and do it all in love.

## Biblical Lessons in Action

- What is your go-to method for showing love to your son? How might you love your son in even more meaningful ways?
- Can you describe your love for your son? How can you put your feelings into words that will have an impact on him? How can you make sure he knows about God's infinite love for him?
- Have you discussed with your son what makes him feel loved? If so, were you surprised by his answer? Is there a different love language you should try? What makes you feel loved by God?

- In what area of showing love are you the weakest? What can you do to get better? How does knowing about God's love help you be a more loving parent?

## PRAYER

Father, open my eyes to see my son with your love and compassion. Grant me wisdom that I might know how best to show him my great love. Help me to love him unconditionally and forgive me when I fall short. Help me teach him how deeply he is loved by you. Amen.

# RESOURCES

Find more information about raising sons with these additional resources.

## Books

*Parenting: 14 Gospel Principles That Can Radically Change Your Family* by Paul David Tripp

*Write It on Their Hearts: Practical Help for Discipling Your Kids* by Chris and Melissa Swain

*Family Discipleship: Leading Your Home Through Time, Moments, & Milestones* by Matt Chandler and Adam Griffin

*The Good Dad* by Jim Daly

*First Time Dad: The Stuff You Really Need to Know* by John Fuller

*Raising Boys: A Christian Parenting Book: A Practical Guide to Faith-Based Parenting* by Quinn Kelly

*So God Made a Mother* by Leslie Means

*Moms Raising Sons to Be Men: Guiding Them Toward Their Purpose and Passion* by Rhonda Stoppe

*Raising Kids to Follow Christ* by Lee Ann Mancini

*Raising Sons and Loving It!: Helping Your Boys Become Godly Men* by Gary and Carrie Oliver

*Boy Mom: What Your Son Needs Most from You* by Monica Swanson

# Articles

focusonthefamily.com/parenting
sarahtitus.com/30-biblical-ways-to-raise-godly-children
christianparenting.org/sons

# Podcasts

*The Christian Parenting Podcast* with Steph Thurling
*Let's Parent on Purpose* with Jay Holland
*Parenting Today's Teens Podcast* with Mark Gregston
*Dear Mattsons* with Jeff and Terra Mattson
*The Monica Swanson Podcast* with Monica Swanson
*Rocking It Grand* with Chrys Howard and Shellie Rushing Tomlinson

# ACKNOWLEDGMENTS

To the four J's who made us parents. Jeremy, Jenifer, Jeb Daniel, and Jessica. You are our greatest treasures, and we love you dearly! You are so precious, and words can never express how blessed we are to be your parents. We thank God for you daily, and we appreciate your never-ending support on our writing journey.

To our extra blessings, Adam and Dawson. We're so glad God added you to our family as sons-in-love. Thank you for being godly husbands, for loving our daughters, and for taking such good care of our grandkids.

To our moms. Thank you for teaching us what it means to be parents. We treasure our family trees and are very thankful for you.

To all those special people who've helped us raise our children, because we didn't do this alone. For our church family: thank you, beloved pastors, ministers, Sunday school teachers, children's and student and college leaders who taught our kids what it means to follow Christ. For extracurricular mentors, like scout leaders, sports coaches, guitar instructors, and dance teachers: thank you for the huge role you played in raising children of strong faith and good character. And for dear friends: thank you for being additional moms and dads to our sons and daughters– we love you big!

To our agent, Cyle Young: thanks for everything!

To Penguin Random House: a huge thank-you for another project that we've enjoyed immeasurably. We're incredibly thankful for this opportunity and for every person who helped this book become reality. You're amazing!

Lastly, but first in our lives, to our Heavenly Father. *We've tasted and seen—YOU ARE GOOD!*

# ABOUT THE AUTHORS

**David and Julie** met in a 10th-grade chemistry class, and sparks flew right away! High school and college sweethearts, the two married after graduation and began work on their master's degrees. Julie received a master's degree in early childhood education, and David's master's in entomology followed his biology undergrad degree.

With diplomas in hand, David joined the navy as a medical entomologist and Julie continued teaching public school. Over the next 20 years, Julie and David lived in 10 different homes as David's career took them to Florida, North Carolina, back to Florida, Virginia, California, Washington, and finally landing in their home state of Georgia.

By the time David retired from the navy and started work as a wildlife biologist for an army installation, the couple had added four children to the family—two boys and two girls. At the birth of their first child, Julie became a stay-at-home mom and part-time freelance writer. Julie and David homeschooled their four children through high school, and their four favorite humans are now college graduates.

Oldest son Jeremy works as an elementary school counselor. Jenifer, an executive administrative assistant, is married to Adam Sartain, a senior marketing manager, and the two are parents of Benaiah and Maverick. Jeb holds a financial analyst position in the aerospace industry. And Jessica, a seminary event planner, is married to Dawson Goddard, a seminary student and sixth-grade Bible and history teacher, and they are the parents of Danae.

With David retiring last year, Julie and David are enjoying more time with their children and grandchildren, loving the opportunity to spend more time outdoors, and finding lots of time to write together. They are the authors of books, magazine and newspaper articles, and devotions.

Their most favorite hats to wear? Mommy and Grandmommy, Daddy and Granddaddy.

Hi there,

We hope *Raising Good Sons* helped you. If you have any questions or concerns about your book, or have received a damaged copy, please contact customerservice@penguinrandomhouse.com. We're here and happy to help.

Also, please consider writing a review on your favorite retailer's website to let others know what you thought of the book.

Sincerely,

The Zeitgeist Team